THE MANX CA...

THE REMARKABLE STORY OF ALFRED CURPHEY SQUIRE OF BALLAMOAR

JOHN CANNAN

Loaghtan Books
Caardee, Dreemskerry Hill
Maughold
Isle of Man
IM7 1BE

Published by Loaghtan Books

First published: June 2022

Copyright © John Cannan 2022

Typesetting and origination by:
Loaghtan Books

Printed and bound by:
Short Run Press

Website: www.loaghtanbooks.com

ISBN: 978-1-908060-36-5

Photographic copyright © John Cannan 2022 unless otherwise indicated

All rights reserved. No part of this publication may be reproduced, stored on a retrieval system or transmitted in any form or by any means without prior permission of the publishers.

A big thank you to my wife Irene for all her love,
support and patience.

Front cover: The only known photograph of Alfred Curphey, Squire of Ballamoar, together with two of his conquests, Nora Mellon (top) and Lady Vivian

Rear cover: Ballamoar today (courtesy of Mike Clague and with permission from Mrs Pamela Shimwell-Mayo)

Title page: Ballamoar House and Garden as Alfred Curphey knew it (courtesy of Ray Stanfield/Les Clarke)

CONTENTS

Chapter 1	Drama at the Ritz	4
Chapter 2	The Early Years	7
Chapter 3	A 'Good' Marriage	9
Chapter 4	A Robber Baron falls in Love	13
Chapter 5	A Cuckoo in the Nest	16
Chapter 6	The Squire of Ballamoar	19
Chapter 7	An Aristocratic Scandal	23
Chapter 8	The Bubble Bursts	26
Chapter 9	The Cuckoo Returns	28
Chapter 10	Upholding an Englishman's Honour	30
Chapter 11	The Fugitives	33
Chapter 12	Financial Ruin Again	35
Chapter 13	Our Man in Mexico	36
Chapter 14	In the Army now	40
Chapter 15	The Financier's Daughter	43
Chapter 16	A Philanderer is Cuckolded	46
Chapter 17	A Mystery to the End	47

ACKNOWLEDGEMENTS

The genealogical websites www.ancestry.co.uk and www.findmypast.co.uk proved very useful in sourcing information from census records, details of births, marriages and deaths, lunatic asylum records, passenger lists, British Army records and British newspaper reports.

Records of Bankruptcy and Liquidation cases were found through *The Gazette* at www.thegazette.co.uk.

Copy of birth and death certificates for Alfred George Curphey were obtained from the General Register Office for England and Wales. His marriage certificates along with papers relating to his two divorces are on record at the National Archives in Kew. A good deal of information was obtained from the UK National Archives at Kew and I am exceedingly grateful to my friend Eileen Sanderson who painstakingly photographed pages and pages of information for me in respect of records that are not available online.

Information from Isle of Man newspapers comes from the Imuseum facility www.imuseum.im run by Manx National Heritage.

Much of the information surrounding the Mellon divorce and the involvement of Alfred Curphey comes from the book *Mellon – An American Life* by David Cannadine (First Vintage Books edition February 2008).

Extracts and reports from American newspapers are courtesy of www.chroniclingamerica.loc.gov

The historical images of Ballamoar and other Isle of Man locations have been kindly provided by Les Clarke and Ray Stanfield.

Various other sources have provided small but important details to the story:

Peter Kelly from the Isle of Man Victorian Society for information on Ballamoar Castle.

Mike Clague of Michael Heritage Trust for use of some of his photographs of interiors of Ballamoar and Mrs Pamela Shimwell-Mayo, the current owner of Ballamoar, for allowing these images to be used.

Henry Clay Frick papers from the Frick Collection at the Frick Art Reference Library, New York

Heliopolis: Rebirth of the City of the Sun by Agnieszka Dobrowolska and Jaroslav Dobrowolski (2006) for information on developments in Egypt in the early 20th Century.

Historic Pittsburgh: www.historicpittsburgh.org for information on the hotel Schenley in Pittsburgh.

Epsom and Ewell History Explorer: www.eehe.org.uk for information on British Army medical classifications in World War 1.

BBC News: '100 years after the 1907 credit crunch' for information on the impact of that financial crisis on business interests in Egypt.

CHAPTER 1

DRAMA AT THE RITZ

The Ritz-Carlton hotel in New York opened on Madison Avenue in Manhattan in December 1910. The first hotel of the upmarket Ritz-Carlton franchise to be opened outside of Europe it vowed to bring English and Continental style to the United States. From the outset it was a place to see and be seen. In April 1912 it would provide a place of sanctuary to J Bruce Ismay, owner of the White Star Line, after he was brought ashore from the Carpathia having been rescued from the sinking of the Titanic. Known for its service and its cuisine it would also find fame when Louis Diat, a chef at the restaurant, was credited with the invention of vichyssoise soup.

Since opening, there had been little to disturb the refined air of genteel service other than some controversy about women being allowed to smoke in public rooms within the hotel and gentlemen being refused access to the dining room unless they wore evening dress. Those arriving in morning attire were directed to the grill room. The management of the hotel denied this was hotel policy but rather a standard preferred by the vast majority of their guests.

Thursday 15th June 1911 therefore proved to be a rather more eventful day at the hotel than might have been anticipated. As guests settled down to an early dinner between 5 and 6 pm, thick smoke began to circulate through the hotel. The telephone switchboard operators were inundated with calls from concerned residents and the smoke soon became so bad that the diners were forced to flee the dining room, many holding napkins over their mouths.

Staff at the hotel searched the premises in vain to locate the source of the fire within the building. Eventually a pile of rubbish was found to be burning on land adjacent to the hotel producing copious quantities of acrid smoke. The hotel had large ventilation fans in the wall at fifth floor level and these proved an excellent conduit to take in the smoke and distribute it round the hotel. The fire brigade swiftly dealt with the fire and the hotel began to return to normal, albeit suffering smoke damage variously estimated at between $5,000 and $10,000. As things transpired the fire was not the only event at the hotel that was to create newspaper headlines the following day.

The Ritz-Carlton hotel, New York, scene of the arrest of Alfred Curphey on 15th June 1911

At around the time of the fire, two English gentlemen, reportedly army officers, along with other residents at the Ritz-Carlton were standing outside the hotel on the corner of Madison Avenue and 45th Street, very possibly having left the premises to escape the smoke. The two were Alfred George Curphey and Captain Thomas Kirkbride. They were surprised to receive a tap on the shoulder from two men claiming to be detectives from the New York Police Department and to be told that they were under arrest for contempt of court and obstructing public justice. Having established that the two detectives, Messrs Curry and Raftis were indeed genuine, they were shown a telegram stating:

'T.W. Kirkbride and Alfred George Curphey at the Ritz-Carlton. Have been indicted in Alleghenny County for obstructing public justice and contempt of court. Arrest and hold for requisition. Agent with papers will arrive tomorrow morning.'

The men were accused of ignoring a subpoena in Pittsburgh, Pennsylvania and of fleeing to New York. Alfred George Curphey had been named as co-respondent in the divorce case of Andrew W Mellon and his English wife Nora Mellon (née McMullen).

It transpired that it had not been difficult for the detectives to identify Curphey and Kirkbride as they were helped by two anonymous men from Pittsburgh who just happened to be in the vicinity. Without further fuss the two men agreed to accompany the detectives to Police Headquarters. En route they managed to get word of their arrest to their lawyers, Thomas W Churchill and J Norris Miller of Miller, Hornblower and Potter.

At Police Headquarters they were soon joined by lawyer George Gordon Battle of O'Gorman, Battle and Lindsay. He had with him a telegram from the District Attorney of Pittsburgh authorising him to act in the matter and requesting that the men be held on very substantial bail. It appears to be more than coincidence that Mr Blakeley, the District Attorney of Alleghenny County, Pennsylvania was known to act in a private capacity for Andrew Mellon, the plaintiff in the divorce action.

To the lieutenant at Police Headquarters Alfred Curphey stated that he was 39 years old, born in the Isle of Man and single. His American address was care of the Ritz-Carlton Hotel. Captain Kirkbride said he was a resident of London, 40 years old and a Captain of the Reserve in the British Army.

The police had wanted to place the men in cells but their lawyers successfully argued to defer this action and a long search for someone to stand bail began. This was proving to be unsuccessful with close to twenty people being proposed only for them to refuse or not be contactable. Among those mentioned was the multi-millionaire Henry Phipps, who was claimed by Curphey to be a close personal friend but he too proved not to be available.

The only known photograph of Alfred George Curphey. It is believed to have been held amongst the Mellon divorce case papers

By this time it was getting late and following a telephone request, Judge Malqueen agreed to a special hearing at the Democratic Club and this hearing was convened at 10.30 pm. There was considerable wrangling between the various legal counsels with Mr Battle claiming that there was a strong risk that they would seek to flee the country for England and the charge was not believed to be one on which they could seek extradition. Mr Miller for Curphey argued that there were no sailings to England the following day and Mr Kirkbride added that as a British Army officer he was honour bound not to flee. Mr Battle's reply was that there were boats to other places and trains to Canada and that Mr Kirkbride had already fled from Pittsburgh!

Judge Mulqueen appeared to have some sympathy with the Englishmen. They declared that they had gone to Pittsburgh voluntarily as a result of the scandalous allegations made in the divorce proceedings. They agreed that they had received the subpoena but it had ordered them to appear at the offices of a private law firm, the one acting for the other side, rather than before a court which would be the practice in England. They therefore travelled to New York at the request of their own lawyers to discuss matters.

Tombs prison, New York

The Judge was also perturbed by the timing of the arrest which had occurred after bonding and surety companies had closed for the day thus making it difficult for defendants to find bail.

Nevertheless the Judge was obliged to honour the subpoenas and bail was set at $2,500 each. It was only after midnight that bail was arranged and a night in the cells at Tombs prison for both parties was avoided. A contemporary newspaper report from the *New York Tribune* of 16th June 1911 indicated that bail was put up by George Considine, the proprietor of the Hotel Metropole. If so then it is likely that the bail amount was subsequently taken on by a recognised bail or surety company. The incident was widely publicised in the New York press, across the United States and in England. In general there seemed to be considerable sympathy with the plight of the two Englishmen. The events did not receive a mention in the press in Pittsburgh, the power base and home of Andrew Mellon.

Quite why Captain Kirkbride was included in the subpoena is unclear. He was indeed an officer in the British army with the rank of Captain in the Royal Horse Artillery. The involvement of Alfred Curphey was quite a different matter. He was not an officer in the army although he probably would have done little to correct the newspaper reports in this regard. It was not the first time he had been economical with the truth in what was a quite extraordinary life.

CHAPTER 2

THE EARLY YEARS

It is likely that Alfred Curphey's early childhood cannot have been easy. His origins were far removed from the glitz and glamour of places such as the Ritz-Carlton. In spite of the details he gave upon his arrest in June 1911, he was actually born in Wallasey, Cheshire on 25th March 1872. He was the youngest child of Samuel Curphey and Georgina Curphey née Pearce and had two older sisters, Esther Eva and Mary Edith.

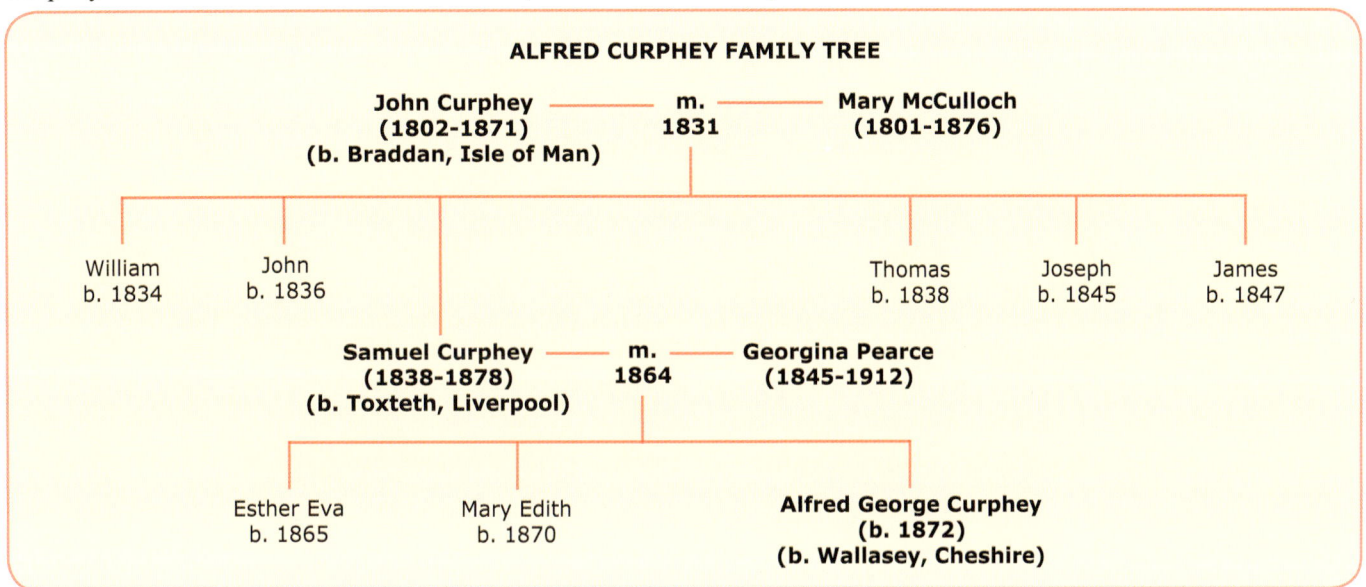

Curphey is a name of Manx origin but his father was born in Toxteth, Liverpool in 1838. Alfred's Manx ancestry goes back to his paternal grandfather John Curphey who was born and lived in Braddan before moving to Liverpool following his marriage to Mary McCulloch in 1831. Alfred's father and grandfather were both joiners by trade.

Samuel Curphey appears to have suffered mental problems, possibly alcohol related and in what was a less enlightened age he was confined in a lunatic asylum on two occasions. On the first occasion he was an inmate at the Chester Lunatic Asylum (later the Countess of Chester hospital). He was admitted on 7th February 1872 just over a month before Alfred was born and was released on 15th November 1872 when he would see his new born son for the first time. He was admitted as a pauper and was noted as 'recovered' in the asylum's record books.

Sadly Samuel's recovery was not permanent and he was readmitted to the lunatic asylum, this time Rainhill in Prescot on 23rd April 1877, just after Alfred's fifth birthday. This time there was to be no recovery and he died in the asylum on 9th December 1878, aged just forty.

It cannot have been easy for Samuel's widow, who was now left to bring up 3 young children on her own. Esther, the oldest, would have been just 13, Mary 8 and Alfred only 6. As a result she had to make some hard decisions. The two girls were sent to live with Georgina's older brother Joseph and his wife Margaret. Joseph was a master shipwright by trade and he and Margaret appear to have brought the girls up as their own. Certainly in the 1881 census the girls are listed as Esther Pearce and Mary Pearce and are living with Joseph and Margaret and their son Arthur at 1 Victoria Road,

Extract from birth certificate for Alfred George Curphey

Waterloo in Liverpool. As a master shipwright Joseph was obviously reasonably wealthy. The house, which is still there in Waterloo, is substantial and Joseph employed a domestic servant Mary Baxter so presumably had the wherewithal to ensure that the two girls were well looked after.

Georgina made what must have been a difficult decision to leave the girls with her brother in Liverpool and move the length of the country to Sussex to take up the post of housekeeper for Eric Williams, the headmaster of a private school in Arundel Road, Brighton. She took her young son Alfred with her. The 1881 census shows Georgina as being the housekeeper at the school in Brighton, with Alfred being shown as a scholar at the same school. It seems to have been a relatively small private school in a building that is still there in Arundel Road just off Brighton seafront. In addition to Eric Williams and Georgina there were a cook, domestic servant and one tutor by the name of John Russell teaching a handful of pupils ranging in age from 9 to 17. At just nine years old Alfred was one of the youngest pupils.

Whether the reason for her move to Brighton was originally work related or not, a relationship developed between Georgina and Eric Williams and they were married in 1883 when she was 37 and Eric just 26.

It is likely that despite the distance between them that Georgina kept in touch with her two girls. Esther married a tobacconist called John Grimshaw but Mary appears not to have married. In the 1911 census Georgina is recorded as a 'visitor' at 35 Lawson Road, Colwyn Bay. The property is described as a House of Rest and her younger daughter Mary is also listed as a visitor at the same address in the 1911 census. Georgina died there the following year.

In addition to being a schoolmaster, Alfred's stepfather Eric Williams, also gave elocution lessons. Later he would give up teaching and make a name for himself in the early years of the film industry. In a way he could be seen to be a pioneer of the talking pictures. He would arrange to make films of dramatic scenes from Shakespeare sometimes appearing in them himself. He would then record the dialogue to be played in conjunction with the film thus giving every appearance of the film being a 'talkie'.

By the time of the marriage of Eric Williams and Alfred's mother in 1883, the school was no longer operating in Arundel Road. The premises had been taken over by a builder and decorator. Whether the school had moved premises or had closed, by 1891 Eric is listed as the proprietor of Grafton House school in Worthing. In any event, for young Alfred the move to Brighton was to provide him with something that would prove invaluable, namely a good education. Given that his stepfather gave elocution lessons it is very likely that Alfred would also have known how to 'talk proper'.

CHAPTER 3

A 'GOOD' MARRIAGE

By 1891 Alfred was 19 years old and the census of that year records him as a lodger at a boarding house run by a Mary Hathaway at 3 Stafford Place in London and his occupation is given as a surveyor and land agent's assistant. He must already have had some financial means at his disposal as Stafford Place in the Victoria district was and remains an upmarket area, located only a stone's throw from Buckingham Palace. While the road remains, there is no longer any evidence of number 3 as there has been substantial redevelopment.

Where he was working is also not clear although there is later evidence that he was in partnership with Peter Purves, an established land agent from Huntingdonshire so it is possible that he started out as an assistant to Peter Purves and then progressed to going into partnership. In 1892 a partnership between Peter Purves and James J Done was dissolved so it is conceivable that Alfred was then able to go into partnership in place of Mr Done. Certainly contemporary newspaper advertisements feature the names of Purves and Curphey land agents during the period 1895 to 1897. By 1898 the advertisements are in Alfred's name only with a telephone number of 345 West suggesting both a parting of the ways from Peter Purves and a degree of success and affluence.

Press coverage from 1902 about an objection to the routing of the railway through land near Padstow in Cornwall reveals that Alfred Curphey was the owner of the land and objected to the proposed route passing through it. It is reported that he had bought the land some time ago for building purposes but no housing had yet been built on the land. His objection was not sustained and the railway was built on the proposed route. Presumably his connections as a land agent had helped in his purchase of this land but he also had to have had the financial means to buy it.

The source of at least some of his affluence may be due to the fact that he had entered into what might have been termed at the time a 'good' marriage. On 15th June 1893 he was married at the parish church in Sutton, Surrey to Grace Dundas Hamilton Souter Robertson, daughter of Stewart Souter Robertson, one time chamberlain to the Duke of Hamilton and his wife Ann. Alfred's address is given as 3 Stafford Place, Buckingham Gate, London and his profession as surveyor.

St Nicholas's Church, Sutton. The parish church where Alfred Curphey married Grace Robertson. (Photograph © George Hobbs)

The marriage certificate gives perhaps the first indication that Alfred was not adverse to being somewhat economical with the truth. His age is listed as being 26, the same age as his bride, although he had only just turned 21 at the time of the marriage. Quite why he felt this lie about his age to be necessary is not clear. At 21 he was legally able to marry without parental consent. Perhaps it was seen as more socially acceptable for the groom to be the same age as his bride rather than 5 years her junior. He might also have lied about his age from the outset of his relationship with Grace and now had to maintain the pretence. Presumably such details were not checked thoroughly in those times.

On the same certificate his father is named but listed as gentleman with no indication that he had died, perhaps to avoid his new in-laws being able to enquire too deeply into his family background.

These little subterfuges would tend to indicate that the groom's side of the church might not have had any of his immediate family in attendance. There is no evidence as to whether or not he was still in touch with his family. In the 1891 census his mother is still in Sussex but had she been at the wedding it is less likely that he would have been able to show an incorrect age on the marriage certificate. He is even less likely to have kept in touch with his sisters, having been separated from them at the age of six. In the 1891 census Esther is shown as married to a tobacconist John Grimshaw and living in Huyton, Liverpool. Mary was unmarried and still living in Waterloo with her, now widowed, aunt.

Alfred's progress in business and his marriage to a well-connected family certainly seems to have helped open up access for him into London's society. Grace's sister Mary had married Edward de Segundo in 1891. Edward, a witness at Alfred and Grace's wedding, was an accomplished electrical engineer, who had been enrolled as a member of the Association of Civil Engineers in 1889 and was clearly building a successful career. For a period of time Alfred shared offices with Edward de Segundo at 28 Victoria Street in London.

Connections to the de Segundos appear to have further helped Alfred's acceptance in high society and he is listed in 1895, along with Mrs de Segundo (his sister-in-law) as attending a garden party given by Lady Ellis at her home Buccleuch House in Richmond. The guest list as reported in the Morning Post on 25th May 1895 was extensive with numerous members of the English aristocracy in attendance along with high ranking military figures and their wives. The guest of honour was the Marchioness of Salisbury, president of the Ladies Grand Council of the Primrose League. She was also the wife of Lord Salisbury who shortly after would become prime minister, his third time in the role.

The Primrose league was an organisation formed to promote Conservative principles in Great Britain and had been founded in 1883. Clearly any memories of Alfred's poor working class beginnings had long since been consigned to the distant past.

In 1897 he is initiated into the St Mary's lodge of the Freemasons. It is also likely, either through his business interests or through his connections with the de Segundos that he became acquainted with one or more members of the McMullen family, owners of a substantial brewery business in Hertfordshire.

John McMullen was also an electrical engineer and so likely to have come into contact with Edward de Segundo and thus possibly Alfred. Some of John McMullen's brothers were also likely to have encountered Alfred at some point. Howard and Alexander both appear to have lived life in the fast lane and to have run up considerable gambling debts. Another brother Leonard had at one time been head brewer of the family business but had been dismissed for drunkenness and was later listed as being a stockbroker. Despite his latter occupation, he appears to have had little ability to manage his finances. It is probable therefore that Alfred would know Nora, the younger sister of the McMullen brothers. Nora was seven years younger than Alfred based on his real age rather than the one stated on his marriage certificate.

The newly married Curpheys settled down to live in London, first at 4 Holden Terrace, Victoria Street then at Albert Chambers in Victoria Street and later at Queen Anne Mansions by St James's Park. All these addresses are in upmarket areas of London. Queen Anne Mansions, built by Henry Alers Hankey in the 1870s were at one time the tallest residential building in London reaching to 14 storeys. It was reported that Queen Victoria had objected to the building as it obscured her view of the Houses of Parliament from Buckingham Palace. Tenants had to be of the 'highest respectability'. The mansions were demolished in 1973 and the other buildings where they lived have also been demolished or altered out of all recognition.

In the 1901 census Alfred is listed as living at Queen Anne Mansions but there is no mention of Grace. This might have been because she was out of the country at the time. She is not traceable in the 1901 census records and she was known to travel to France to pursue her love of painting. It might also, however, be the first indication that all was not well with the marriage.

In divorce papers first filed in 1904 it was stated that Alfred had left the family home between 5th and 6th September 1903 and had withdrawn conjugal rights from his wife. It was likely that there had been problems much earlier than this. In the various letters in the divorce proceedings where Grace has asked him to return to her so they can live as man and wife, mention is made of his affair with a lady named Alice. Grace does not mention the lady's surname. Alfred's one time partner Peter Purves had a younger sister called Alice who was just five years older than Alfred. She could therefore be the Alice named although there is no further evidence other than the coincidence of the name. That things had become bitter between husband and wife is obvious from the divorce correspondence with Grace accusing him of spending all her money and then denying her funds. In turn Alfred accused the de Segundos of turning her against him.

In any event the differences were irreconcilable and a decree absolute was granted in 1905 on the grounds of desertion and adultery with an unknown woman. The adultery cited in the case was said to have occurred on two occasions, firstly on 2nd June 1905 at the hotel Metropole in Brighton and then again on 9th June 1905 at the Charing Cross hotel in London. It is possible that the adultery cases were used to speed up the final process of the divorce but what is known is that, in the latter years of their marriage at least, Alfred had been anything but faithful.

CHAPTER 4

A ROBBER BARON FALLS IN LOVE

Andrew W Mellon would be given many labels during his lifetime. These included banker, industrialist, businessman, Republican politician, avid art collector and philanthropist particularly with regard to the arts. Son of Thomas Mellon, an Irish immigrant who had carved out a successful business career in Pittsburgh, Pennsylvania where he established the bank T Mellon & Sons, Andrew was one of eight children although three died in infancy or early childhood and was the fourth of the five surviving brothers. Andrew displayed an astute ability for business and under his stewardship the Mellon business expanded considerably diversifying from banking into many areas of industry, notably aluminium as well as oil, steel, shipbuilding and construction.

By the 1920s he was reportedly one of the highest paying taxpayers in the United States behind only J D Rockefeller and Henry Ford. He subsequently branched into politics serving as Secretary of the Treasury under three different presidents from 1921 to 1932. He later served as the US Ambassador to the United Kingdom from 1932 to 1933 before retiring. He died in 1937 aged 82.

One of the less flattering titles given to him along with several others was that of 'robber baron', a term applied to several US businessmen of the late 19th and early 20th century who it was felt acquired great wealth by exploiting natural resources and people and who were not averse to using unscrupulous methods to achieve their aims. Andrew Mellon certainly wielded considerable power and influence in Pittsburgh and wider Pennsylvania and was quite prepared to use this to his own ends. One title that would seemingly also be applied to him was that of confirmed bachelor. As he reached his forties he was still unmarried and living in the parental home at 401 Negley Avenue in Pittsburgh. While he undoubtedly had the wherewithal to move into his own place he seems to have had no inclination to do so, preferring to concentrate on his business interests. Indeed he seems to have lived quite a reclusive life outside of business circles and would try to avoid social functions where possible. All this would change in 1898 when Andrew, then aged 43, fell hopelessly in love.

Along with his lifelong friend and fellow businessman Henry Frick, Andrew embarked on one of his frequent trips to England on the White Star liner Germanic. On board Frick introduced him to Mr and Mrs McMullen and their 19 year old daughter Nora. The McMullens were returning from a round the world trip. The father Andrew McMullen ran the McMullen brewery in Hertfordshire that is still in existence today and the family lived at Hertford Castle as tenants of Lord Salisbury.

Andrew Mellon pictured in 1921

Nora Mellon née McMullen

Nora was the youngest child and only daughter of a large family and was undoubtedly indulged by her parents and older brothers. Despite the considerable age gap Andrew and Nora seem to have got on well together to the extent that Andrew was invited to stay with the McMullens at Hertford Castle during his time in England. It is hard to imagine how a relationship developed between the taciturn American businessman and the young, naive English girl from the shires but Andrew seems to have displayed a charming nature hitherto rarely seen and Nora found him interesting and easy to talk to. While not in the same league as the Mellons, the McMullens were a wealthy family but were more inclined to spend their money than accumulate it. Several of Nora's brothers were known to spend in excess of their income on a regular basis. Two of the brothers were regularly in trouble for running up gambling debts.

The extravagant wedding of Andrew and Nora Mellon took place at St. Andrews church in Hertford on 12th September 1900

Following Andrew's return to Pittsburgh, he and Nora kept up a regular if rather formal correspondence and when Andrew returned to England the following year he was resolved on marrying Nora and proposed to her that summer. Nora politely but firmly declined stating that while she was flattered by his proposal, she did not believe they would be happy. It was not only a matter of the age gap but the two lived in quite different worlds with seemingly little in common. Nora's father was also known to have reservations about the suitability of the match, however wealthy his prospective son-in-law might be. Andrew was not prepared to take no for an answer and continued to correspond with Nora following his return to Pittsburgh. By early 1900 their correspondence was becoming more obviously affectionate and when Andrew visited England in Spring 1900 Nora relented and accepted his proposal. With the marriage date set for September of that year Andrew returned again to Pittsburgh where he bought a house at 5052 Forbes Street in East Liberty and proceeded to furnish it and engage staff to run it, seemingly without involving Nora in any of the arrangements.

Andrew returned to England in August 1900 along with friends and relatives and there were several stag parties arranged by his brothers as well as receptions by various art dealers keen for Andrew's patronage. H J Heinz, founder

of the Heinz canned food empire was among those attending the stag parties. The wedding itself was a lavish affair and took place on Wednesday 12th September 1900 at St Andrew's church in Hertford with the bride and groom then departing to Europe on honeymoon. The honeymoon trip took them to Germany and France but it is clear that Andrew was still much preoccupied with business matters and their trip to Berlin was principally arranged so as to allow Andrew to hold a business meeting with regard to Union Steel. By early October 1900 they were in Paris, by which time Andrew was clearly eager to get back to work in Pittsburgh. Shortly afterwards they make a brief visit back to Hertford before leaving Southampton for New York on board the St. Louis of the American Line. From New York they wasted no time before taking the train to Pittsburgh.

Despite the fact that she had been on a round the world tour with her parents, Nora had led a relatively sheltered existence. She was, therefore, ill prepared for the industrial landscape that greeted her as they approached Pittsburgh and she was undoubtedly shocked to discover that her future home was in the middle of the city rather than a country estate. Her reaction when their train pulled into Pittsburgh station and Andrew stood up to disembark was reportedly 'We don't get off here, do we? You don't live here?'

She found it difficult to get on with Andrew's family and dinners at his parents' home must have been particularly difficult for a gregarious young woman as the meals were conducted almost completely in silence. All a far cry indeed from the life she had enjoyed in Hertford. Almost inevitably she was homesick and feeling isolated and lonely. Andrew, however, appears to have been oblivious to all this, believing them to be blissfully happy. All things considered it was a far from auspicious start to married life.

By the time the couple settled into their new home at 5052 Forbes Street in November 1900, Nora was already pregnant and their first child, a girl named Ailsa was born on 28th June 1901. As was the custom of the time for wealthy families, a nurse by the name of Miss Abernethy was immediately engaged to look after the baby. With a nurse in attendance and Andrew spending lots of time at work Nora would find the days long with little to occupy her time and few opportunities in Pittsburgh to enjoy the outdoor pursuits such as horse riding that she had pursued back home. While it is always difficult to judge the marriage of two people from the outside, the different expectations of the two parties seemed like a recipe for future trouble.

CHAPTER 5
A CUCKOO IN THE NEST

In the late summer of 1901 the Mellons travelled to England no doubt to show off the new baby to Nora's family. Regular summer trips to England were made throughout their marriage. Nora also did not lack for material things as Andrew was known to buy her jewellery from New York, London and Paris even though such extravagant spending on these types of things was not the normal Mellon practice.

In February 1902 Nora was forced to return to England for a much sadder reason, having received notification that her father Alexander McMullen was dying of cancer. Andrew was unable to accompany her as he was heavily involved in the launch of Mellon National Bank at the time. Nora arrived in Hertford just in time to see her father before he died and after the funeral she returned to New York on board the SS *Philadelphia* in March 1902. She was accompanied on the voyage by her mother. Travelling on the same vessel was Alfred George Curphey.

Alfred Curphey was on the voyage with James P Scott, who came from Philadelphia, and Alfred was ostensibly travelling with Scott to Pittsburgh on business. As mentioned previously whether Alfred was already known to Nora is likely but not entirely clear. It seems an extraordinary coincidence, although not impossible, that they would first become known to each other on board ship and were both travelling to Pittsburgh. On balance it is more likely that they already knew each other. One of Nora's brothers was an electrical engineer and so is likely to have known Alfred's brother in law Edward de Segundo and his family. It is also possible that Alfred was known to the McMullens through his business as a land agent. Later American newspaper reports would state they were childhood friends although it is more probable that he knew her as a young girl by association through her brothers. In any event Nora introduced Alfred to Andrew Mellon when he met her in New York and persuaded him to invite Alfred and James Scott to dine with them at their home in Pittsburgh. For Andrew Mellon it would come to feel as if he had invited a cuckoo into the nest.

In June 1902 the Mellons left for an extended stay in England. They would be there until September. They visited Paris and London but spent most of the time at Hertford so Nora could be with her recently widowed mother. They met occasionally with their new friend Alfred Curphey and dined with him or went to the theatre while up in London. Andrew Mellon visited Curphey's offices in Victoria Street and bought from him two coach horses that Nora had much admired. At Andrew's expense Alfred arranged for the horses to be shipped to America. Ironically Andrew named them Curphey and Cope (after another friend of Alfred).

In March 1903 Alfred Curphey was back in New York and once again made contact with the Mellons. He advised Andrew that he had

The SS Philadelphia *where Alfred Curphey and Nora Mellon coincidentally made acquaintance*

several business ventures on the go, including coal lands in West Virginia and a patent for electric railway signals, but that he was temporarily in need of funds and asked for a loan of $20,000. Remarkably Andrew agreed seemingly without making too many enquiries into Alfred's business background. The loan was due to be repaid at the beginning of April. Nora invited Alfred to stay with them in Pittsburgh for a while and they later met with him in New York where they went to the theatre and for dinner.

At the beginning of April Alfred was unable to repay the loan and Andrew Mellon duly extended the repayment terms. By the time Alfred returned to England on 1st May 1903, on board the SS *Etruria*, the loan had still not been repaid.

In June 1903 the Mellons were all set to embark on board the *Orcana* from New York to Liverpool when fate intervened. Henry G Morse, who founded the New York Shipbuilding Company, collapsed and died from a stroke. Andrew Mellon, who along with Henry Frick, provided much of the finance for the venture was forced to stay behind to sort things out. Nora travelled on to England without him along with her daughter Ailsa and the nurse Miss Abernethy. With Alfred Curphey's help she found a house to rent called Sandlea at Datchet, near Windsor.

St. George's Chapel, Windsor, the scene of illicit trysts between Alfred and Nora. (Photograph © Aurelien Guichard)

Alfred seems to have been a regular visitor and it was not long before the amount of time he was spending with Nora attracted attention. Nora's brother Leonard warned Nora that gossip was circulating that she had been seen around town with Alfred Curphey and that he was known to be of dubious character. Given that Leonard had been fired from the family brewery business for drunkenness and was often known to be in financial difficulties, it is likely that he knew more about Alfred's character than many. Nora immediately told Alfred who reportedly threatened Leonard with a thrashing although they never came to blows. Even after Andrew Mellon belatedly arrived in England, Alfred Curphey was still a regular visitor. The repayment date for Alfred's loan again fell due and once again he was unable to pay so it had to be extended. It is difficult to understand how such a hard-headed and successful business man as Andrew Mellon could have been so easily persuaded to extend credit in this way. Alfred Curphey must indeed have had a persuasive manner and put up a convincing front.

As the divorce papers for Alfred's separation from Grace would reveal in September 1903 he moved out of the family home and it seems that over the winter of 1903 he kept up a secret correspondence with Nora Mellon. In June 1904, just as the Mellons were about to embark on their regular visit to England, Nora dropped a bombshell. She announced that she wanted to divorce Andrew and go to live in England with Alfred Curphey. During the course of the journey Andrew believed that he had persuaded her not to proceed with such a mad idea but he could not have been more wrong.

As the Mellons arrived at their London hotel Andrew was surprised to see Alfred Curphey at dinner seated at a nearby table. It was presumably not a surprise to Nora. Shortly afterwards the Mellons moved to the house near Windsor where they planned to spend the summer. Word soon reaches Andrew that Nora and Alfred Curphey were seen having a clandestine meeting at St George's Chapel, Windsor. For Andrew this must have been the final straw and he confronted Alfred Curphey at his offices in London.

Alfred confessed his love for Nora and admitted he knew it was wrong stating that, if only his finances were not in such a parlous state, he would go to South Africa so as to remove himself from the temptation of trying to see Nora. Andrew informed Nora that Alfred Curphey was clearly a fraud but Nora repeated her desire for divorce and retired to bed with an unspecified illness stating that her distress and illness were in part caused by Alfred Curphey's poor financial state. No doubt prompted by Alfred she told Andrew that the Curphey ancestral home at Ballamoar on the Isle of Man

Ballamoar House and garden. The original farmhouse was demolished to make way for a palatial new residence. (Photograph courtesy of Ray Stanfield/Les Clarke)

was about to be seized for non payment of debts. Ever the businessman Andrew Mellon spotted the possibility of a deal and the means to get Curphey out of their lives. He made enquiries and discovered that Ballamoar was indeed connected to the Curphey family. Unfortunately his enquiries did not go so far as to realise that Alfred had no connection to this particular Curphey family. With further urging from Nora, Andrew agreed to pay Alfred Curphey money, ostensibly to redeem the debts on the family home but in reality a payoff to get rid of Alfred Curphey from their lives once and for all. Andrew demurred when he discovered that the amount requested was £20,000 rather than dollars (the exchange rate at the time was about $4.87 to £1) but ultimately agreed and on 1st July 1904 the money was transferred to Alfred's account at Barclays bank in London.

The Mellons subsequently returned to Pittsburgh, seemingly reconciled, with Andrew confident that he had seen the last of Alfred George Curphey.

CHAPTER 6

THE SQUIRE OF BALLAMOAR

What was Alfred Curphey going to do with his new found riches? It seems that his claim that he needed the money for his 'ancestral' home was not too far off the mark. At the end of August 1904 he purchased 1,200 acres of land at Ballamoar in the parish of Jurby on the Isle of Man. The land purchased included the derelict house that had been the home of the Curphey family.

Despite the same name there appears to have been no connection between the Curpheys of Ballamoar and Alfred's family. The Curphey family had been at Ballamoar for generations before the house passed to the Farrant family upon the marriage of Susanna Curphey to William Farrant in 1822. How Alfred Curphey came to hear about the house and the link to the Curphey name is not known. His grandfather John Curphey had died the year before he was born and he was only six years old when his father died. As he then moved with his mother to Brighton, he is unlikely to have had any connections with other members of his own Curphey family. Most likely the proposed sale of the estate came to his attention through his business as a land agent in London and the link to the name Curphey had surfaced at this point. Certainly the details for the sale of the estate in 1903 had attracted a good deal of interest, including it was reported, several English investors.

In any event the property was purchased from the Isle of Man Bank for the sum of £14,500 and extensive plans were put into action to demolish the former building and build a new palatial home on the site. For this purpose Alfred engaged the services of a London architect by the name of Harold W Crickmay. A report in the Mona's Herald dated 3rd August 1904 reported that the estate extended to 525 acres with the property being in fair condition except the mansion house and gardens. At the same time Alfred Curphey also bought two further estates in the North of the Island from a gentleman from Cumbria by the name of John Burnyeat for £10,525.

Ballamoar. Although the original building was demolished the gardens had already to some extent been established by the Farrant family. (Photograph courtesy of Ray Stanfield/Les Clarke)

Despite now being a wealthy man, it appears that Alfred had no intention of paying off any historical debts. In the New York Tribune of 31st December 1904 it was reported that the sheriff had made an attachment of £11,500 on property owned by Alfred Curphey in London on behalf of the Western Pocahontas Coal and Lumber Co. This company

The imposing entrance gates to Ballamoar (Photograph courtesy of Ray Stanfield/Les Clarke)

was based in the coalfields of West Virginia, the adjoining state to Pennsylvania and only around 100 miles from the centre of Andrew Mellon's business operations in Pittsburgh. Andrew Mellon's business interests certainly included coal so there may have been some connection. By 1905 Alfred had other matters on his mind as the divorce decree from his wife Grace had been served on him in May.

At the beginning of 1906 work was progressing on his new estate at Ballamoar on the Isle of Man and he was a regular visitor to the island staying at the Mitre Hotel in the nearby town of Ramsey. The arrival of the new wealthy resident attracted interest in the local press, particularly the *Ramsey Courier* and his various activities were regularly reported. It is doubtful that he made any mention on the Island of any possible connection to the Curphey family who had previously been connected with Ballamoar. This was a well known Northern family and any attempt by Alfred to hint at a connection would not have stood up to close scrutiny.

The scale of the work at Ballamoar and the seeming extravagance of the money being spent on this substantial property continued to be avidly reported by the local press. The *Ramsey Courier* dated 31st August 1906 stated that a housekeeper and four manservants had now arrived. It also commented on some of the expensive materials being brought in to the Island for the work. This included 40 tons of ashphalte (sic) together with a gang of men and associated machinery from London

Example of wood carving on cupboard panelling in the porch at Ballamoar. The work was undertaken by the local firm of Kelly and Sons. (Photograph courtesy of Mike Clague, Michael Heritage Trust, and with permission of Mrs Pamela Shimwell-Mayo)

Right: Baron Edouard Empain, the developer of Heliopolis and a major shareholder in the Egyptian Mail Steamship Co. Ltd
Below: Heliopolis c. 1910: the grand scheme of Baron Empain to develop a garden city on the outskirts of Cairo

for the work. It also noted that 30 tons of Yorkshire stone was to be used for paving in front of the residence. Work undertaken on the interior was no less extravagant. A local firm entitled Kelly and Sons were engaged to undertake joinery work and they also produced numerous fine wood carvings such as the cupboard doors in the entrance porch with supposed likenesses of the early kings of Mann. By the end of August work at Ballamoar was close to completion and it was reported that he would be taking up residence there shortly. He had also seemingly turned his interest to new business ventures, in particular investment opportunities in Egypt.

Egypt was seen as offering exciting opportunities at the beginning of the twentieth century. One of the most grandiose schemes was the development of the garden suburb of Heliopolis, the dream of the wealthy Belgian Baron Edouard Empain. With the assistance of Boghos Nubar Pasha, the son of the Egyptian Prime Minister, Baron Empain had a vision of a massive new development to be called Heliopolis and called it 'a city within a city'. Nowadays wholly within the urban sprawl of Cairo, Heliopolis was originally some distance from Cairo and the elaborate scheme included a tramway system connecting the new development to the centre of Cairo.

Amongst the companies associated with the development and controlled by Baron Empain was the newly formed Egyptian Mail Steamship Company Limited. Formed in 1906 to run a reliable service from Marseille to Alexandria, the Egyptian Mail Steamship Company Ltd had an impressive list of wealthy subscribers. Baron Empain subscribed to 4,000 ordinary shares and 3,500 deferred shares while Boghos Nubar Pasha held 6,000 ordinary shares and 5,250 deferred shares. Another notable investor was Lord Armstrong of Bambergh Castle in Northumberland. William Watson-Armstrong had inherited a great fortune from his great uncle Lord Armstrong in 1900 and was the director of the North Eastern Railway Company. He was a known philanthropist and in 1901 had donated £100,000 to found the Royal Victoria Infirmary in Newcastle on Tyne.

Another major subscriber of 4,000 ordinary shares and 3,500 deferred shares was Alfred George Curphey of 5 Bury Street, St James, London. Alfred Curphey, listed as 'gentleman' was also shown as one of the directors of the company. Alfred Curphey was moving in very wealthy and influential circles.

Two other investors and directors were Major Charles Hyde Villiers and George Todd Symons, a shipowner. Major Villiers and George Symons seem to have made representations to the Home Office to allow the word 'Royal' to have been included in the company title in view of the fact that they were seeking to secure the mail contract for the service to Egypt. In this they were not successful and the company was incorporated without the word 'Royal' in the title.

Top: SS Heliopolis. *The* Heliopolis *along with its sister ship SS* Cairo *were built for the Egyptian Mail Steamship Company by Fairfield Engineering of Govan on the Clyde.* Heliopolis *was later renamed the* Royal George
Above: *first class cabin on SS* Heliopolis

The company had commissioned the building of two new steamers to provide the service. The ships were built by Fairfield Engineering on the Clyde. They were speedily built. Both ships, the SS *Cairo* and the SS *Heliopolis* were launched in 1907 and entered service at the end of that year.

A through service by train and ferry was advertised from London Charing Cross via Calais then on to Marseille with fares of 12 guineas for first class and 9 guineas for second class. The journey was advertised as taking 4 days. Notable passengers included a 17 year old Agatha Mary Clarissa Miller, later to become well known as the renowned crime author Agatha Christie travelling with her mother Clara to spend the winter months of 1907/08 in Egypt. The famous composer Giacomo Puccini was also known to have used the service.

CHAPTER 7

AN ARISTOCRATIC SCANDAL

By any standards the years 1906 and 1907 appear to have been good years for Alfred Curphey. His substantial residence at Ballamoar was completed along with several other significant land purchases in the North of the Island. The *Ramsey Courier* continued to report avidly on the newly arrived rich and flamboyant individual in their midst. His regular visits to and from his new mansion were eagerly reported as were various examples of his largesse.

Brasier Tourer MN33 belonging to Alfred Curphey near Ramsey pier. The driver is almost certainly his chauffeur while the passenger is very likely one of his Egyptian associates. (Photograph courtesy of Ray Stanfield/Les Clarke)

A keen dog show enthusiast he donated silver cups to the Ramsey Dog Show, winning several himself. He was also reported as having donated £25 to the poor of the parish of Jurby and to have offered £1,000 towards the restoration of Jurby parish church. He also became a committee member for the Ramsey Bay regatta. It seems he was enjoying the life of a local celebrity and living up to the unofficial title bestowed upon him by the *Ramsey Courier* of the 'Squire of Ballamoar'. The same newspaper was also proposing that he would be a fine prospective candidate to stand for the House of Keys (the Manx government) in the Sheading of Ayre at the next election. Apart from having hitherto shown no interest in politics, it is likely that Alfred Curphey would not have encouraged this type of speculation as it would doubtless have necessitated a more in depth scrutiny of him and his background than he would have found comfortable. A later suggestion that he might be a suitable candidate to replace Hall Caine, the famous writer who was at that time considering resigning as member of the House of Keys for Ramsey also seems not to have gained credence.

While some of his generosity may have seemed focused towards supporting his unofficial role of 'Squire' within the community there is also evidence that he was not adverse to genuinely philanthropic actions. In September 1907 there was an accident at Ballamoar which resulted in a groom suffering a broken arm. He was treated at the local Cottage hospital in Ramsey. On hearing that the Cottage hospital did not have an X-Ray machine Alfred Curphey promptly arranged to buy one for the hospital. This was again reported in the *Ramsey Courier* of 4th October 1907, no doubt as Alfred intended but it was nonetheless a generous gesture.

In the latter months of 1907 Alfred's exploits continued to be followed eagerly. Local schoolchildren were entertained to tea at Ballamoar in October. In November he was in a box at the Gaiety theatre for a performance by the Douglas Choral Union. On 3rd December he was to be found along with Lord Armstrong on board the SS *Heliopolis* as it made its trial run through the Irish Sea from Govan to Plymouth. Ever one for the flamboyant gesture he sent a Marconigram to the *Ramsey Courier* from onboard, the message reading 'Rosslare Radio. To *Ramsey Courier*, Ramsey, Isle of Man. *Heliopolis* passes the Island this evening. Delighted to find several Manxmen are afforded employment on board. Curphey of Ballamoar'.

Everything in Alfred's garden seemed rosy but it was all about to unravel quite dramatically. The first hint of trouble was a summons for Alfred Curphey dated 18th December 1907 commanding him to appear before the Consular Court at Cairo on 21st December 1907 in respect of a claim for monies owed to a gentleman by the name of Emile Thubron. Thubron was well known in the world of motor boat racing but also ran an engineering and boat building business in Cairo. The claim against Alfred Curphey was for £E 233 – 15s plus interest and commission of £E 70 – 6s – 6d and costs of £E 20. At that time the Egyptian pound was more or less equivalent to the pound sterling. Whether Alfred was aware of the court claim or not (he presumably knew he owed money to Thubron), he was not in Egypt at the time. He also had other things to occupy his mind.

Invited guests at Ballamoar. Although Alfred Curphey was known to entertain local schoolchildren to tea, this image probably dates from the coronation celebrations of George V in June 1911 by which time Alfred was no longer the owner. (Photograph courtesy of Ray Stanfield/Les Clarke)

Lady Vivian. Wife of the Boer War hero the 4th Baron Vivian

On 13th November 1907 a Hollandtide concert had been held at Ballaugh Parish Hall under the patronage of A G Curphey Esq of Ballamoar, Jurby along with Lady Vivian, David Croall Esq and Ernest Long Esq. Lady Vivian had been a constant companion of Mr Curphey during his time at Ballamoar and was regularly to be seen riding her horses through the countryside. Together with Alfred Curphey she was a regular prize winner at local dog shows. Anyone wondering who the mysterious Lady Vivian might be was about to find out. On 21st December 1907 the divorce proceedings between Lord Vivian and his wife Lady Vivian were reported extensively in the English newspapers. Alfred George Curphey was named as co-respondent. Details of the proceedings were also eagerly reported in the Manx newspapers although there was no mention in the *Ramsey Courier*.

George Crespigny Brabazon Vivian, the 4th Baron Vivian was educated at Eton and joined the 17th Lancers where he served with distinction in the 2nd Boer War. He was wounded at the Battle of Elands River in September 1901. On 1st August 1903 he married Barbara Cicely Fanning at St. Michael's Church, Pimlico. The couple had two children, Daphne born July 1904 and son Anthony born March 1906. All seems to have been well until the couple returned from Canada in October 1906. Lady Vivian had agreed to take part in some theatricals at the Royalty Theatre. Lord Vivian had objected to this feeling it was not befitting for a lady of her stature. Certainly in Edwardian England those involved in the theatre were often seen to be somewhat lacking in morals.

Lady Vivian deferred to her husband's wishes and later that winter the couple travelled to Egypt. In Cairo Lord Vivian had arranged to go on a shooting expedition but was concerned that his wife had made the acquaintance of Alfred Curphey while they were in Cairo. Lord Vivian had made enquiries and felt that Curphey was not a desirable person for his wife to know. At Lady Vivian's insistence he went on his shooting trip but on his return he found to his dismay that his wife had continued to keep company with Curphey and some of his friends.

The couple began their return journey to England but Lord Vivian was taken aback when his wife announced that she would be leaving the ship at Marseilles and joining a motoring party, which included Alfred Curphey, to drive back through France. She would have been the only lady in the party and it was only when Lord Vivian spoke directly to Alfred Curphey that the proposed motor tour was abandoned. The disagreement between the couple was not resolved, however and upon returning to England Lady Vivian announced that she would no longer live with her husband as his wife. In April 1907 she left the family home. Upon returning from a trip to America Lord Vivian found that his wife was living in the Isle of Man with Alfred Curphey. On 25th October 1907 a somewhat contrived situation seems to have been arranged whereby Annie Smith, Lady Vivian's maid was asked to arrange for Lady Vivian's luggage to be taken to the Euston hotel where a room had been booked in the names of Mr and Mrs Curphey. The maid further reported that the following morning, while doing her ladyship's hair, Alfred Curphey appeared in his dressing gown. Two private investigators were also on hand to witness all of this so it seems likely that the whole process had been engineered to facilitate the divorce proceedings. Lord Vivian was granted a *decree nisi* and custody of the two children.

Lord Vivian would remarry in 1911, this time to Nancy Lycett Green and had two further children with his new wife. Given his earlier history with his divorce from Grace and dalliance with Nora Mellon this type of scandal was unlikely to have caused any great concern to Alfred Curphey. The same is probably true for Lady Vivian. For Alfred Curphey, however, things were about to get considerably worse.

CHAPTER 8

THE BUBBLE BURSTS

From 1903 to 1906 the global economy had boomed but 1907 would see this boom end in a financial crisis. A lot of problems stemmed from a lack of liquidity in the markets. For Britain the coffers had been drained by the Boer Wars and there had been huge payouts from Lloyds of London to cover insurance losses from the San Francisco earthquake in 1906. One of the casualties was the Egyptian Stock Market which suffered a severe crash necessitating a shipment of 3 million dollars in gold to bail it out. The global crisis was relatively shortlived but the crash in the Egyptian market had ramifications for businesses with interests in Egypt. One such casualty was the Egyptian Mail and Steamship Company Ltd. On 7th July 1908 a notice in the London Gazette stated that the company was no longer able to meet its obligations and was to be placed into liquidation.

Wealthy individuals such as Baron Empain and Lord Armstrong were no doubt able to ride out the storm but the impact on Alfred Curphey would have been considerable.

In early January 1908 rumours that Mr Curphey would be leaving Ballamoar for an extended period were denied. In an article published in the *Isle of Man Times* on 25th January 1908 Alfred Curphey outlined plans to drain the wetlands in the North of the Island known as the Ballaugh Curraghs and create an extensive market garden to provide fresh fruit and vegetables for sale on the island and in the North of England.

On the same day as the article was published Alfred Curphey and Lady Vivian were detained as they were about to board the boat to Liverpool. The reason for the detention was not specified other than it was a pressing matter. It does not take too much of a stretch of imagination to think that the matter probably involved unpaid debts. The sailing departure was unusually delayed by a few minutes and the two were allowed on board, presumably having reached some form of agreement with those seeking to detain them. It would be the last that the Isle of Man would see of Alfred George Curphey.

Alfred's financial situation would seem to have deteriorated rapidly in 1908. Despite the large sum of money he had received from Andrew Mellon, he had lived a very extravagant lifestyle. He had a mortgage on Ballamoar and had borrowed significantly to purchase shares in the Egyptian Mail and Steamship and other Egyptian companies, using the shares themselves as security against the loan. It all came to an inevitable conclusion and in May 1909 Alfred George Curphey of 5 Bury Street, St James, London was declared bankrupt.

The *Ramsey Courier* does not appear to have mentioned this at the time but other Manx newspapers were not so reticent. The *Mona's Herald* of 9th June 1909 had an extensive feature on the former resident, an extract from which is worth reporting as it not only provides detailed information of his financial affairs but also indicates that Alfred was still not averse to being economical with the truth.

'A sitting was held on May 26th, in the Court of Bankruptcy, London before Mr Registrar Gifford, for the public examination of Mr Alfred George Curphey described as of Bury Street, St James's', SW. The liabilities were returned at £18,725 of which £10,660 is expected to rank against available assets £75. – In answer to Mr W.P. Bowyer, Official Receiver, the debtor said that from 1889 to 1904 he was in business as a surveyor and valuer in Victoria Street, Westminster. In 1904 he went to America where a friend, whose guest he was, gave him an interest in a syndicate. At the end of three months he returned to England, having received £45,000 as his share of the profits of the syndicate. He next went to Egypt and early in 1905 became a partner in a firm of bankers and brokers in Cairo, whose business was shortly afterwards taken over by the Belgian Company styled the *Societe Generale Egyptienne pour l'Agriculture et le*

Commerce. He was given a large number of shares in the *Societe* and acted as a director of it until the end of 1907 when he resigned.

He was also interested, both as shareholder and director in several other companies, including the Egyptian Mail Steamship Company Ltd, which was registered in England for the purpose of running steamers between Marseille and Alexandria. He and his associates guaranteed a subscription of £440,000 out of the capital of £660,000 and he had taken 4,000 shares of £10, for which he paid cash, borrowed for the purpose from the *Societe* on the security of his shares and other securities deposited with them. Whilst in Egypt he speculated largely in stocks, shares and land and in 1905 and 1906 made considerable profits, more than sufficient to justify his expenditure at the time of about £6,000 a year. In 1907, a financial crisis occurred in Egypt, which seriously depreciated his holding in various companies. Soon afterwards the Egyptian Mail Steamship Company Ltd failed, whereupon his shares therein, became absolutely valueless and he lost the whole of the £40,000 which he had invested in that company. In addition to other securities deposited with the *Societe* he lodged with them the £40,000 shares allotted to him in the Steamship Co. He had not received a final account from the *Societe* but he believed that matters were about even between them. In 1905 he purchased 1,500 acres of freehold land near Ramsey, Isle of Man and erected there a residence at a total outlay of £48,000. At the time of the Egyptian crisis the *Societe* sold the property for £45,000, which was placed to his credit in the account with them. His failure was entirely the result of the crisis and the collapse of the Egyptian Mail Steamship Co. Ltd.

The examination was concluded.'

It is interesting to note that Alfred's version of how he came by his wealth in 1904 was through a friend, whose guest he was, giving him an interest in a syndicate in America! It is unlikely that Andrew Mellon would have had the same view on this. Presumably the Official Receiver was less concerned with where his money had come from and more on where it went and what was left.

The sale of Ballamoar took place quite quickly having been completed by March 1908. Interestingly enough the buyer was Francois Rom who was a director of the bank holding the mortgage. Francois Rom did take up residence at Ballamoar and lived there for several years until after the outbreak of World War 1. He was noted for trying to provide a refuge for Belgian refugees who had fled the advancing German army.

In terms of the bankruptcy it was clear that the liabilities far exceeded any assets and it was no surprise that the bankruptcy was concluded in February 1910 with unsecured creditors, including some on the Isle of Man, only receiving 5/8 of 1d in the pound.

CHAPTER 9
THE CUCKOO RETURNS

While his financial woes had been painfully exposed to public scrutiny, Alfred Curphey was not one to worry over this and it is unlikely that he lay awake at nights worrying about the people that he had left unpaid. After they had left the Island in January 1908 it seems that it was not long before he and Lady Vivian parted company. Lady Vivian followed her long held desire to go on the stage but her career was shortlived and she married John Douglas Faskally in December 1908 and the couple moved to Biarritz in South West France. This marriage, like her first, was not destined to last and in 1912 she abandoned her husband and their child and ran off with a gentleman by the name of Luis de Ugarte. Her second marriage therefore also ended in divorce in August 1913 and she did subsequently marry Luis de Ugarte. Alfred also did not waste any time. What was he to do to restore his life to the style to which he had become accustomed? The answer was once more to seek out Nora Mellon.

Much of the information about Alfred's movements and actions over the period 1908 to 1911 come from papers presented to the court during the divorce case between Andrew and Nora Mellon. A lot of it comes from a deposition to the court from a gentleman called Charles Ernest Long and his testimony is mentioned often in coverage of the divorce proceedings. Long was a friend of Alfred Curphey and had been living at Ballamoar where he was described as acting as Curphey's agent. He is mentioned along with Alfred Curphey, Lady Vivian and David Croall as being guests of honour at the Ballaugh Hollandtide concert in 1907. By 1911, however, the pair had fallen out and in December 1911 the reason became clear when Long successfully sued Alfred Curphey for the return of certain plate, furniture and pictures or the value thereof. These items had been brought to Ballamoar by Long following the death of his mother but they had subsequently been pledged by Curphey as security against debts. Long would be successful in the court with judgement being that he was to be paid £1,532 or £50 if the goods were returned to him in proper condition within 14 days. It might be supposed therefore that Long's deposition to the Mellon divorce proceedings would not be designed to paint Alfred Curphey in a good light.

The Mellon family travelled over to England in May 1908 and stayed at a house called Park Close near Windsor. In June 1908 Nora Mellon went on holiday to Paris with her friend, the actress Maxine Elliott. Andrew was reluctant to let her go but agreed. The plan had been for Andrew to join her in Paris but Nora persuaded him it was not worth the upheaval for the short time they would be there. At the same time she asked Andrew to grant her a permanent regular allowance. The reason behind her suggestion that Andrew did not join her and the request for a regular allowance rather than Andrew just paying for everything as she went along would soon become clear. In Paris Nora had met up again with Alfred Curphey. The meeting is likely to have been engineered and managed by Alfred but there was no doubt that Nora was not happy within her marriage. The Mellons' second child Paul had been born in June 1907 but Nora was soon restless and looking for a means of escape. Once again she hoped that Alfred Curphey would provide her with the excitement that was so clearly missing in her marriage to Andrew. Alfred Curphey was no doubt only too happy to oblige, particularly if Nora had independent means thanks to a regular allowance from her husband.

Andrew initially suggested an annual allowance of $10,000 but Nora felt this to be inadequate and they finally settled on $25,000. Even while in London with Andrew in the summer of 1908 Nora reportedly used a variety of excuses to meet up with Alfred Curphey, including days she went to London to sit for the portrait that Andrew had commissioned for her.

In mid-September 1908 the Mellons returned to Pittsburgh together with Nora's widowed mother Mrs McMullen. After a three month stay Nora accompanied her mother back to England in December and spent Christmas there while Andrew and the children stayed in Pittsburgh. According to Long when Nora returned to the United States in January 1909 accompanied by two of her sisters-in-law, he and Alfred Curphey were also passengers on the same sailing registered under the names of E. Long and C. Long. It seems that Nora had confided her love for Alfred to her sisters-in-law and they had agreed to keep her secret allowing her and Alfred to consort openly while on board the ship. By this time Alfred was living at 5 Bury Street, St James with the rent no doubt paid for from Nora's allowance. This was the address given at his bankruptcy hearing later that year, the same hearing at which he stated that he was now living on assistance from friends.

While Nora was enjoying her transatlantic tryst with Alfred Curphey, Andrew Mellon's mother had died. He had telegraphed her with the sad news and was waiting to meet her when the ship docked at New York. Nora was reportedly agitated and nervy when Andrew met her and to his eyes not very solicitous with her condolences as might be expected. She was anxious to travel immediately to Pittsburgh to collect the children but was probably also worried that her husband and her lover might meet on the quayside. According to Long, he and Alfred remained in New York staying at the Majestic Hotel on Central Park West before taking rooms on 68th Street. Showing Maud and Gee, her sisters-in-law the sights afforded Nora with the opportunity to meet up with Alfred Curphey knowing that her secret was safe. Although also in New York with her, Andrew was kept busy with work matters giving Nora chances to meet up with Alfred. In early March she took Maud and Gee to see Niagara Falls and persuaded Andrew not to accompany them. The three women stayed at the Iroquois hotel in Buffalo where Alfred Curphey and Long also stayed.

The Majestic Hotel in New York was demolished in the 1920s to make way for a new building but it had been an impressive 600 room luxury hotel featuring a bowling alley amongst other features. Famous residents include the composer Gustav Mahler, who may well have been there at the same time as Alfred Curphey and a young Dorothy Parker. The Iroquois hotel has also disappeared but was described as being a symbol of modern opulence and luxury. Given that Alfred had no funds of his own available and would shortly be facing a bankruptcy hearing in England, it would seem that he was able to stay in such grand surroundings because Nora was paying the bills from her allowance from Andrew. It is ironic that his bankruptcy hearing was adjourned from April to May because he was staying in luxurious surroundings in the US on the day that the hearing in London was originally scheduled.

Andrew and Nora took Maud and Gee to California onboard a private railcar which meant this time Curphey or Long could not tag along. By the time they return to Pittsburgh, however, Alfred is there staying at the Hotel Schenley. Today the Hotel Schenley is part of the University of Pittsburgh campus but in 1909 it was an exclusive place to stay and a place to dine on 'haute cuisine'. Information from the Historic Pittsburgh website shows that when opened in 1899 the Hotel Schenley was Pittsburgh's first skyscraper hotel and became known as the 'Waldorf of Pittsburgh'. It was built by the Bellefield company which included Andrew Mellon amongst its stockholders.

It seems strange that up to this point Andrew Mellon was unaware that Nora had once again met up with Alfred Curphey. While the pair might have enjoyed relative anonymity in New York or Buffalo, it must have been much harder for them to meet up in Pittsburgh where the Mellon family were so well known and where there must have been people who would have been happy to report any apparent scandalous goings on to Andrew. The fact that Alfred was staying in probably the most prestigious hotel in Pittsburgh, indirectly at Andrew Mellon's expense seems both an audacious and insolent move.

On the morning of Easter Sunday (11th April 1909) Nora told Andrew that Thomas Chadbourne, his long time friend and a local lawyer would be calling on him later that day. Seemingly after much prevarication Chadbourne told Andrew that Nora had made an irrevocable decision to leave him and that she wished to seek a divorce and go back to live in England. To Andrew this news reportedly came like 'a bolt out of a clear sky'. Given that she had asked for a divorce in 1904 he must have convinced himself that this was firmly in the past and all was well. No mention at this juncture was made of another man. It would be his brother Dick Mellon who would tell him that almost certainly Alfred Curphey had returned.

Perhaps wisely Curphey and Long had left Pittsburgh by this point and on 20th April 1909 they arrive in Liverpool from New York on board the *Mauretania*. Alfred would go back to London to face his bankruptcy hearing no doubt quietly confident that his money troubles would soon be over.

CHAPTER 10
UPHOLDING AN ENGLISHMAN'S HONOUR

The Mellon divorce was a lengthy process that became increasingly acrimonious. Nora's 'shock' announcement left Andrew Mellon with a problem. It was a time when divorce was still very much frowned upon, especially in strong Presbyterian areas like Pittsburgh. It was characteristic of the Mellon family that they avoided publicity wherever possible and he would have been well aware that a divorce from his wife would attract unwelcome public attention.

With a frosty atmosphere at home, any reconciliation became increasingly unlikely. Andrew reportedly offered to leave Pittsburgh and live elsewhere if that would make Nora happy. How genuine this offer might have been is uncertain as it seems unlikely that Andrew Mellon would move from the power centre of his business empire and long term home of his family. It became academic anyway as Nora was set upon divorce and both parties engaged lawyers.

In a demonstration of the power of money Andrew dispatched detectives to London and Europe with letters of introduction from the chief of detectives in Allegheny County to the chief of Scotland Yard and from the acting US Secretary of State to US embassies and consular officials. Their purpose was to find out if Nora had been involved in an adulterous affair.

Conclusive proof of this would prove difficult to find and in the summer of 1909 a legal separation was agreed with a view to the dissolution of the marriage on the grounds of desertion after two years. Nora received a generous initial settlement of $250,000 and alternating custody of the two children was agreed. In August 1909 Nora departed for Europe having reportedly given an undertaking that the children would have no contact with Alfred Curphey while they were with her. She is reported to have said that due to her own family's dislike of Alfred Curphey she had decided she no longer wished to be associated with him. Whether she said this or not it would soon become clear that it was not meant in earnest.

At first, however, she seems to have been true to her word. She initially settled in Paris and it was there that Andrew brought the children to her. Alfred Curphey was not there. Indeed Andrew had discovered that Alfred was leaving for South Africa and arranged for a detective to travel on the same sailing to ensure that Curphey was in fact on board.

Quite why Alfred had gone to South Africa is not clear. Passenger lists do show that Alfred Curphey departed Southampton for South Africa on board the Union Castle Steamship Company liner *Saxon* on 4th September 1909. It was presumably a business trip although how this was financed by a man in the middle of bankruptcy proceedings is hard to fathom. The most obvious answer is that Nora Mellon had provided the means although given his past history it is possible that he had secured money from others on the pretext of an extravagant business venture.

In any event Alfred's absence is shortlived. On 31st December 1909 Alfred George Curphey is again listed as a passenger on board the liner *Saxon* returning from South Africa to Southampton. From there he went to Paris to be with Nora. As the children were still with her at the time it seems her promise to keep them away from Alfred Curphey was shortlived. Once again Andrew Mellon hired detectives to watch Nora's activities with Curphey. Nora was aware of this and was no doubt careful to be circumspect in public.

On 23rd March 1910 the children returned to Pittsburgh with Andrew via Southampton and New York on board Kaiser Wilhelm II. Nora meanwhile crossed to England and took a six month lease on a property at Vale Farm near Windsor with Alfred. On 31st May 1910 Nora is listed on board the *Caronia* sailing from Liverpool to New York as she travelled to collect the children. She was accompanied by Captain Kirkbride, Alfred's friend, who would later be arrested with him at the Ritz-Carlton Hotel in June 1911. Alfred would presumably have deemed it unwise to travel to the United States with her and thus stayed at Vale Farm to await her return with the children, Ailsa and Paul.

By mid-June the arrangement was for the children to travel back to England with Nora. Despite assurances from both Nora and her lawyer that Curphey would not be with her when she had the children, Andrew did not believe this to be the case. It was at that point that word reached Andrew from one of his many detective sources that Curphey was ensconced at Vale Farm and that Nora intended to join him there with the children.

So when Andrew accompanied the children to New York for the trip to England he refused to hand them over to the nurse and instead confronted Nora at her hotel about her proposed residence with Curphey in England. An argument ensued and Andrew returned to Pittsburgh with the children. It was eventually agreed that the children could be with Nora but only if she stayed in Pennsylvania. The bizarre situation then arose whereby Andrew vacated his home to allow Nora and the children to live there during July and August while he took rooms at the University Club.

Relations between Andrew and Nora became even more strained to the extent that Andrew, fearing that Nora would abscond with the children to England employed people to keep a watch on her and also went so far as to install listening devices in the house. He also abandoned the previous agreement for divorce on the grounds of desertion after two years' separation and instead sued for divorce on the grounds of adultery.

He immediately hired a large number of lawyers not because he needed such a number but as a tactic to deny Nora access to the best lawyers herself. It was a tactic that he had successfully employed in many of his business dealings.

While all this was happening in Pittsburgh, Alfred Curphey remained in England presumably still living at Vale Farm which was being paid for by Nora and thus indirectly by Andrew Mellon. No evidence has emerged to indicate what he might have been doing to earn any money during his time with Nora. Over the course of his life he had variously claimed to be a land agent, broker and financial agent. While there is plenty of evidence from his early life to confirm his work as a surveyor and land agent there is limited evidence to indicate his business activities following on from the disastrous venture into Egypt. It is possible to imagine that he used his connections to broker various deals and earn commission from this. It is unlikely, for instance that his three month venture to South Africa was purely for a holiday. In the absence of anything concrete, however, this is all just open to conjecture.

Meanwhile in Pittsburgh Andrew Mellon pressed ahead with his action for divorce on the grounds of adultery. This was an action that was not without risk. In Pennsylvania divorce trials were held before a jury and juries were notoriously reluctant to convict in cases of adultery unless there was clear evidence. Despite his best efforts Andrew had struggled to find unequivocal evidence of this. Nora had also discovered the listening device in the family home and was reportedly not adverse to making seriously derogatory comments about Andrew knowing that they would get back to him. The children were removed from the family home and placed nearby with a German governess, while Nora employed detectives of her own to keep tabs on Andrew.

Andrew's next move was fraught with risk and would prove ill advised. Given that he was struggling for conclusive proof of Nora's adultery and the consequent risk that a jury may not decide in his favour, Andrew now took steps to remove the need for a trial by jury. He lobbied strongly for a change in state law to remove the need for a trial by jury and for divorce proceedings to be heard in private by a judge. It is a testimony to the power held by extremely wealthy businessmen at the time that in April 1911, with a minimum of debate and scrutiny the divorce laws were changed so that the right to a trial by jury was to be at the discretion of the court and a jury trial was strictly forbidden where it could not be held without prejudice to public morals.

The press in Pittsburgh was also strictly controlled either under severe pressure from Andrew and his advisers or more indirectly through the knowledge that adverse reporting could jeopardise their viability to continue in business. Reports of the divorce proceedings were limited or non-existent in Pittsburgh. The same could not be true of other parts of Pennsylvania (notably Philadelphia), the rest of the United States or indeed England.

Nora's lawyers seized on this and on 7th May 1911 an extensive interview with Nora Mellon was published in the *North American*, a newspaper printed in Philadelphia. The article made much of the change in the law and the aim of removing a woman's right to a trial by jury. It also referenced the use of spies and listening bugs and made much of Nora's impassioned plea to the women of the state to help her in a fight against 'the combined money-making and law-makers of the state for possession of my children'. In terms of public opinion at least, Andrew's moves to load the dice in his favour had misfired and there was widespread condemnation of his actions. As Nora's lawyers had intended the article reached a wider audience within the US, evoking considerable sympathy for her cause. News also reached England reportedly prompting a question in the House of Commons about the ill treatment of an Englishwoman abroad.

It was in the aftermath of this article and the subsequent sympathy for Nora that in June 1911 Alfred Curphey appeared in Pittsburgh accompanied by Captain Kirkbride. It would seem that Alfred delighted in the favourable publicity and played up to the idea that he had come to the United States to uphold the honour of an English lady and by implication himself. The North American newspaper reportedly played up reports that Curphey 'proposed to thrash him (Andrew Mellon) within an inch of his life'. Alfred paid a visit to Mellon Bank, making sure the newspaper journalist was around to record the occasion, to confront Andrew Mellon. Andrew Mellon was not there, a fact that was probably already known to Alfred. Given all the publicity surrounding the case and Alfred Curphey's appearance in person, it was no surprise, except possibly to Alfred himself that he was served with a summons to appear as a witness at the upcoming divorce proceedings.

The result was that Alfred Curphey and Thomas Kirkbride travelled to New York. Alfred Curphey's version of events was that they had gone to consult their lawyers. The alternative version was that they were fleeing from justice. The result was their very public arrest outside the Ritz-Carlton hotel on 15th June 1911.

CHAPTER 11

THE FUGITIVES

With bail having finally been secured Alfred Curphey and Captain Kirkbride were at least spared the need to spend time in the cells at the Tombs, the New York City prison. Their fate now hung on a decision by Governor Dix as to whether they should be returned to Pittsburgh in respect of the charges on which the subpoena had been served. It was not until 7th July 1911 that Governor Dix made his decision.

By that time there were two applications on which he was asked to pass judgement. The first was the charge on which their arrest had originally been made, namely disobeying a subpoena to appear before a Notary Public at a private hearing in respect of the divorce of Andrew Mellon in Pittsburgh. This was not accepted by the Governor, seemingly on the technicality that the two men had left Pennsylvania by the time they were due to appear in court to answer the writ. The second application charged the two with conspiracy and contempt, alleging that while in the State of Pennsylvania they conspired to defeat the end of Justice by leaving the state and refusing to obey the subpoena. The second application was granted with the Governor stating 'It appearing that the papers submitted in connection with said request for rendition are regarded by the executive authority of the State of Pennsylvania as a sufficient basis in law for such requisition and no evidence being given to contradict the same, a warrant of rendition is hereby granted'. Alton P Parker appearing for Curphey and Kirkbride stated that if the decision was adverse to his clients he would appeal to the United States courts (*New York Times* 8th July 1911).

The newspaper does not report whether Curphey and Kirkbride were in court for the hearing but the likelihood was that they were not there. It is not mentioned in the *New York Times* report of 8th July but later newspaper coverage states that they were scheduled to appear before Judge Mulqueen in the Court of General Sessions on 12th July 1911. Further information is to be found in another New York newspaper, *The Sun* from the following day. 'Following on from the judgement by Governor Dix, the appearance before Judge Mulqueen was to enforce the extradition order. Curphey and Kirkbride were not in court and Assistant District Attorney Johnstone moved that bail of $2,500 each should be forfeited.

Counsel for Curphey and Kirkbride gave no indication as to his clients' current whereabouts but argued that bail had been granted against a charge of obstructing public justice and that Governor Dix had not approved this charge but rather a second one of conspiracy. As a result judgement was reserved by Judge Mulqueen' (*The Sun* 13th July 1911). Their absence from court had clearly alarmed Andrew Mellon and his legal advisors and detectives were sent from Pittsburgh to try and locate them. George Gordon Battle acting for Andrew Mellon is reported as saying that they had not been found and that their own legal counsel did not seem to know where they were (*The Sun* 14th July 1911).

By 24th July it was being reported that Curphey and Kirkbride had fled from Philadelphia by ship to England. Solely based on newspaper reports from the time it does seem as if the hunt to find the fugitive pair was not conducted in a particularly efficient manner. Paul Ache, counsel for Nora Mellon, admitted that he had dined with the pair in Pittsburgh a few days previously, the pair having been spotted and identified by two of the detectives who had identified the pair outside the Ritz-Carlton, New York in June. The same detectives had apparently talked with them. Quite why they could not be detained at this point is not clear but the pair promptly disappeared again.

Reports that they had boarded a steamer to England without being recognised prompted hasty action to try and bring them back. District Attorney Blakely immediately prepared to sail

Governor Dix of New York

for England on the fastest ship available with the view of detaining the pair on their arrival in England. In addition Robert D Doods, a lawyer for one of the firms representing Andrew Mellon, Read, Smith, Shaw and Beal had already gone to London following earlier reports that they had fled to England and he remained there in the event that they would eventually make an appearance. He had been cabled by District Attorney Blakely to watch every available sailing for a sighting of Curphey and Kirkbride and to make immediate plans for their extradition should this be allowed under English law. It was reported that Andrew Mellon would spare no expense in his attempts to bring the fugitives to justice. (*The Sun* 24th July 1911).

It would seem that reports that Curphey and Kirkbride had fled by steamer from Philadelphia were false. In a cunning move they had fled to Canada and presumably laid low there for a few days. Passenger lists record that Alfred Curphey and Captain Thomas Kirkbride were passengers on board the *Royal George* sailing from Montreal to Bristol on 2nd August. It is probably unlikely that Robert Doods would be checking sailings from Canada into Bristol. There is considerable irony in the choice of ship for their escape back to England. The SS *Royal George* was none other than the SS *Heliopolis* which following the demise of the Egyptian Mail Steamship Company had been purchased by the Canadian Northern Steamship Company of Toronto in 1910 and renamed (see page 22). It may have been purely a fortuitous coincidence that led to them being on board this ship but Alfred must surely have allowed himself a wry smile in the knowledge that he was fleeing the clutches of Andrew Mellon on board a ship that Andrew's money had helped to finance.

On 1st August 1911 the National Surety Company which had provided their bail on 16th June was ordered to pay $5,000 for the failure of Curphey and Kirkbride to surrender themselves to the authorities for extradition to Pittsburgh, the pair now being fugitives from justice. Once back in England it soon became clear that neither Alfred Curphey nor indeed Captain Kirkbride had any intention of returning to the United States and putting themselves before the court in Pittsburgh as witnesses in the Mellon divorce. District Attorney William Blakely arrived back in Pittsburgh in mid September 1911. He offered very little comment but had found both Alfred Curphey and Captain Kirkbride at 5 Bury Street, St James in London but, under English law, he was unable either to enforce their extradition or to force a deposition from them. It was more than obvious that neither was going to return voluntarily.

Being unable to cross examine Alfred Curphey under oath in court was clearly a blow for Andrew Mellon in terms of proving the case for adultery but all was not lost. On 29th July 1911 it had been reported that an important witness by the name of Charles Ernest Long had arrived in Pittsburgh to testify in the case. A newspaper report describes him as being 6ft 4in tall and a Boer War veteran and he was there at the request of the lawyers acting for Andrew Mellon (*The Sun* 29th July 1911).

The divorce arguments continued. Despite the evidence from Long and the extensive work undertaken by private detectives, Andrew Mellon's lawyers were struggling to find conclusive evidence of adultery. Nora's lawyers had also been successful in winning the right to a trial by jury which would make it even harder to successfully prove adultery. By this time, however, Nora's resolve had been weakened by the desertion of her lover in her time of need and the two year period for a divorce on the grounds of desertion was almost completed.

So it was that a compromise was reached and a divorce hearing was held in private on 20th and 21st May 1912 with evidence presented relating only to Nora's desertion. On 3rd July 1912 a divorce was granted on the grounds of desertion. Andrew would have custody of the children for 8 months of the year and Nora for the other 4 on the proviso that they were not taken out of Allegheny county without Andrew's written permission or the consent of the court. For Andrew it was a victory but a costly one. Nora emerged with her honour intact insofar as she was not labelled an adulteress but she had been deserted by the man who had been instrumental in bringing about this situation.

Andrew Mellon never remarried. Nora would eventually marry Harvey Arthur Lee, an Englishman several years younger than her in 1923. There is no record that she ever saw or made contact with Alfred Curphey again.

CHAPTER 12

FINANCIAL RUIN AGAIN

Records are sparse relating to Alfred Curphey's whereabouts and activities for the next few years. He would have lost any support from Nora Mellon once he stepped onto the *Royal George* at Montreal in August 1911. We know from the investigation of District Attorney William Blakely that he was living in 5 Bury Street in London upon his return but what he was doing and what was his means of earning money are not known.

The next possible record of him surfaces in August 1913 when an Albert G Curphey is listed as a passenger on the *Royal George* sailing from Bristol to Montreal on 9th August 1913. While the first name is different, the age given equates to that of Alfred Curphey. The list states he is a tourist with intended residence in Canada. While it is impossible to confirm that it was him, he had used this route before. The likelihood that it was Alfred is increased by a report in the London Gazette from November 1913 concerning the bankruptcy proceedings against one Alfred George Curphey.

The Times dated 18th January 1913 had a list of bankruptcy proceedings to be heard in London in Court 6 of the King's Division before Mr Justice Phillimore. Included on the list is the name 'Curphey, A' with creditors being named as De Segundo and another. This would in turn lead to a First Meeting being fixed for 24th November 1913 at the Bankruptcy buildings, Carey Street, London to be followed by a Public Examination at the same place on 17th December 1913. The debtor is named as 'Curphey, A' with address given late of 59 St. James St, London but whose present place of residence the creditors have been unable to ascertain. An adjudication of bankruptcy was made on 6th February 1914 but as Curphey's whereabouts still remained unknown it is likely that the creditors would have obtained little financial reward from the proceedings.

The intriguing part of these proceedings is that one of the named creditors who seems to have initiated the process for bankruptcy is stated as De Segundo. This is an unusual enough name that it can only have been Edward de Segundo who was married to Mary, sister of Alfred's ex-wife Grace. Given that Alfred and Grace had divorced some 8 years earlier in 1905 it is unlikely that Alfred and Edward de Segundo would have maintained amicable contact. This is particularly true as in the divorce papers, Alfred accused the de Segundos of trying to turn Grace against him. One explanation is that Edward de Segundo was pursuing a long outstanding debt that he was owed by Alfred from some time previously. Alternatively he was instigating proceedings on behalf of others, possibly using an old debt as the pretext. This latter explanation might be more likely given that the creditors named in the bankruptcy registers are Edmond Porges and Henri Ricard trading as E Porges et Fils, Paris. Despite the name Edmond Porges was a British born banker. It is likely that Alfred had run up debts with the bank possibly during his time in Paris with Nora Mellon. The register records the act of Bankruptcy as 'With intent to defeat and delay his creditors, departed out of England etc etc.'

In the light of this information it looks very likely that it was indeed Alfred Curphey that was listed as a passenger on the *Royal George* bound for Canada.

CHAPTER 13

OUR MAN IN MEXICO

Throughout his life to date Alfred Curphey seems to have acted with little regard for the moral standards of the day or the effect of his actions on others. He had not been averse to leaving a trail of debts and damaged marriages behind him but in one thing he had been hitherto consistent, a reluctance to face the consequences or put himself in danger.

This makes the next place in which he surfaced all the more remarkable. He was in Mexico. The evidence for this comes from a review in a West Country newspaper entitled the *Western Daily Mail* dated 14th May 1914 of articles published in a journal entitled 'The 19th Century'. A brief reference is made to the fact that one of the articles is entitled; 'Mexico from Within: An English Resident's View,' by Alfred Curphey.

The actual article is a short four page essay that would jar as extremely racist to the modern ear. Briefly it divides the population of Mexico into three distinct categories. Alfred states that 65% of the population is of pure Indian blood, the descendants of the peoples there before the Spanish invasion. These he characterises as 'wishing only to live out their existence in their own way, not caring who governs the country and not wanting the white man's civilization.' The next 20% he characterises as being of mixed Indian and Spanish descent and states that from this section comes the revolutionaries and agitators. The remaining 15% he claims consists of white Mexicans and foreigners and states that they represent the wealth and industries of the country and it is from this section of society that a government should be formed to ensure stability and order. He concludes by stating that if this 15% are reluctant to form a government then the United States should get involved to restore law and order, adding that it would not take too many troops to achieve this even allowing for large numbers opposing such intervention.

An editorial footnote to the article in the 19th Century magazine reads as follows: 'This contribution, by an English resident in Mexico, was taken to the United States for posting, in order to avoid inspection by the Mexican authorities. All letters and telegrams from Mexico are liable to be inspected – hence the difficulty of obtaining reliable information about the condition of the country. It is hardly necessary to state that this article was written before the commencement of hostilities by the United States.'

The hostilities mentioned are likely to be the American naval bombardment, invasion and occupation of Veracruz in April 1914. Mexico during this time was undoubtedly a dangerous place to be with various factions vying for control.

How Alfred Curphey got from Canada to Mexico is a mystery. There were probably not many ships plying a passenger route between the two countries so the more likely option is that he travelled through the United States. This must have carried an element of risk as it was only just over two years earlier that a warrant for his arrest as a fugitive from justice had been issued.

Félix Díaz, a leading figure in the rebellion against the Huerta and Carranza governments during the Mexican Revolution

Presumably he slipped through unnoticed and the furore from 1911 would have died down following the settlement in the Mellon divorce proceedings.

The next reference to him in Mexico is even more astonishing. It comes in a document from 1920 entitled 'Investigation of Mexican affairs – hearing before a sub-committee Parts 18-23 by the United States Senate Committee on Foreign Affairs.' This references a letter written from Pedro del Villar to Félix Díaz. The date of the letter is not specified but an extract is partly reproduced below:

'The matter of the English. Remembering your idea of the necessity of a better understanding with England in the maintenance of peace and a strong government in Mexico. I have endeavoured to approach the English interests. However they have never come out openly, due to the influence of Rabasa over them. But anyhow, I obtained, through Col. Robert, one of the secret agents of the English embassy, who was present at the meeting, and we came to an understanding with Mr Alfredo (sic) Curphey and authority was given to draw up an agreement. I had several meetings with him and with Mr Ellis Ashmead Bartlett, a member of the English army. Gen. Blanquet was also present at some of these meetings. The final outcome was that the English government will hand over to me, through the person or corporation which it deems the most fit, the funds necessary to bring about the absolute triumph of your movement.'

Despite all his subterfuges in marital affairs, it is difficult to imagine Alfred Curphey as a secret agent but seemingly this was what he had become. In the tangled world of Mexican politics and revolutions the English government had not openly supported any one side. This was predominantly due to the fact that 75% of its oil during the first World War was supplied by Mexico and it had no wish to jeopardise this. Félix Díaz was a Mexican politician who had opposed the Huerta government in Mexico that was ultimately deposed in 1915 and was also an opponent of the subsequent regime of Venustiano Carranza that took power in May 1915. Pedro del Villar was a supporter of Félix Díaz who sought US sympathy in March 1914 for a revolution to depose the current Mexican government led by Huerta and instal Díaz as leader of a replacement regime. The proposal received little or no US support. The name Rabasa mentioned in the extract relates to Emilio Rabasa, a member of the Huerta government who had been a Mexican representative at the Niagara Falls Peace conference to resolve the Veracruz incident. It serves to emphasise the complexity of Mexican politics of the time that the General Blanquet also mentioned was Vice President under the Huerta government but an opponent of the Carranza regime.

The various names referenced would suggest that the meetings referred to in the letter took place sometime in 1914. The English were clearly hedging their bets and Alfred Curphey was involved in a very dangerous game indeed. It is probable that neither he nor Bartlett were officially employed by the British embassy so had these clandestine meetings proved embarrassing for British interests in Mexico, any connection of the pair to the British Government would have been officially denied. This could have left Alfred Curphey and Ellis Ashmead Bartlett dangerously exposed.

A brief mention in a letter dated 1918 from Major Berkeley Levett states that Alfred Curphey 'has done and is doing most valuable work under the Ministry of Information'. The Ministry of Information was not formed until 1918 so it was likely that Alfred's work as a 'secret agent' came together from various sources most probably the Foreign Office, the War Propaganda agency based at Wellington House in London and the Secret Intelligence Service, the forerunner of MI6.

The army officer mentioned in the extract from the letter, Ellis Ashmead Bartlett was in fact a war correspondent whose most noted work was about the ANZAC fighting at Gallipoli. As he travelled to the Dardanelles in April 1915 this again points to the fact that the meeting with Alfredo Curphey took place in 1914 or early 1915. As a War Correspondent Bartlett would undoubtedly have had contact with the War Propaganda agency at Wellington House who were keen to keep an eye on what information about the war was being reported. Ashmead Bartlett's reporting of the Gallipoli campaign was severely critical of the conduct of the campaign and ultimately led to the dismissal of the British Commander in Chief, Sir Ian Hamilton. He was therefore not a man just to print what the British Government wanted.

It is hard to imagine Alfred Curphey as a James Bond figure. Like the fictional figure he definitely seemed to have been attractive to the ladies but he had not been involved in any fighting despite not denying any newspaper reports that depicted him as an army officer. The nearest he had got to fighting at this point had been threatening to thrash Nora's brother Leonard and later Andrew Mellon. Neither of which happened.

Quite whether he continued to live in Mexico for some time or not, Alfred Curphey next surfaces when he is named as attending a reception given by Mrs Tarvin at the Willard Hotel in Washington DC on 5th December 1916. Various newspaper reports give his initials as H G or R G but it is undoubtedly Alfred as they list him as being from Mexico. The reception is reported as being given in respect of the introduction (to society) of Miss Mattie Marschall Curd of Louisville, Kentucky. (*Washington Evening Star* 5th December 1916 and *Washington Times* 8th December 1916).

Some of the other guests include the delegates from the Mexican government to the conference held between the US and Mexican governments between September 1916 and January 1917. The conference was convened on several dates and at various different locations, starting at a hotel in New London, Connecticut then moving to Atlantic City, New Jersey and finally Philadelphia, Pennsylvania.

The delegates are named as Senor Luis Cabrera (Minister for Finance in the Carranza government), Senor Y Bonillas, Senor Juan B Rojo and Senor Roberto Pesqueira. Their invitation had come through Mrs Tarvin's son John W Belt who, it was reported, on his return from Mexico was a member of the party that included the Mexican commissioners.

Other than the fact that he was or had been living in Mexico the reason for his invitation is not known. It is possible that he was a friend or associate of John Belt. It was possible that he too was travelling with the same party from Mexico. It is likely that he would know and possibly be known to the members of the Mexican delegation. It also possible that he was there to gather information for the British government and thus continuing in his role as secret agent.

The British were not party to this conference. It was only between the United States and Mexico. The aims of the US were to resolve the issues of incursions over the border by rebels led by Pancho Villa. These incursions had led to an armed entry by US troops under General Pershing in March 1916. The aims of the Mexicans were the removal of the US troops from part of their country. It is quite conceivable that Alfred Curphey was hoping to glean intelligence for the British.

Willard Hotel, Washington DC, the location for a party in December 1916 where invited guests included Alfred Curphey and members of the Mexican delegation

Given that the reception was being given for the innocuous occasion of the introduction of a young lady to society, the guest list seems to have been quite political in nature. Another named guest was Lincoln Steffens, a well known American journalist who was known as a 'muckraker' for his uncovering of corruption in municipal governments. During the period of 1914 to 1915 he had covered the Mexican revolution and was reported to have left wing revolutionary leanings.

The conference talks ended in February 1917 without any conclusive agreement but US troops were subsequently withdrawn in any case as the attention of the United States' President Woodrow Wilson was increasingly drawn towards the conflict in Europe. It was, however, a Mexican connection, namely the infamous Zimmermann telegram that would ultimately lead to the US entry into World War 1. This telegram was intercepted by the British in January 1917 and leaked to the United States. It contained proposals for a military alliance between Mexico and Germany that, if successful would lead to the restoration of Texas, Arizona and New Mexico to Mexico.

Luis Cabrera, Mexican Minister for Finance in the Carranza government

Alfred presumably enjoyed the reception. If he was following the conference then he may not have been too happy when in its final days the conference met in Philadelphia in Pennsylvania. Although it was now over four years since the Mellon divorce scandal, Philadelphia must have felt uncomfortably close to Pittsburgh.

CHAPTER 14

IN THE ARMY NOW

Whether Alfred stayed in the United States for any length of time is unknown. The next reference to him appears in the small print of *The Sun* newspaper of New York dated 21st September 1917 and is a brief list of court proceedings. Alfred Curphey has a judgement against him brought by J Ludy for a debt of $1,043.30. He was back in the familiar territory of owing money.

Quite what the debt was about is not listed and without access to the Manhattan court records for 1917 it is not likely to be possible to find out anything further. Ludy is not a common name but there is one intriguing possibility. There was a Dr John B Ludy, who was a practising dermatologist in Philadelphia at around this time. He is accredited with publication of some scientific articles, one relating to diseases of the scalp and another pertaining to the use of the Wasserman technique in the detection of the venereal disease of syphilis. Whether this was the same J Ludy and whether the debt related to a treatment of any sort is now only open to speculative conjecture.

There is no way of knowing whether the debt was resolved or whether Alfred followed his usual practice of leaving the country but in any event he arrived in England in June 1918 and at the age of 46 applied to join the army.

The upper age limit for conscription had been 41 but this had been increased to 51 by the Military Service (No. 2) act of April 1918. Alfred would therefore have been eligible for conscription unless he could obtain exemption through proving himself to be medically unfit. While it is quite possible that the war might have been over before he would have been called up, Alfred decided to take matters into his own hands and applied to join the prestigious regiment of the Scots Guards. In doing so he looks to have sought assistance from his friends and contacts, most notably Major Berkeley Levett (see page 37).

Berkeley Levett, a major in the Scots Guards was a colourful character in his own right. The son of Colonel Theophilus John Levett, the MP for Lichfield, Berkeley Levett had acquired a reputation as a *bon vivant* and had at one time reportedly been labelled the best dressed man in London. He had become known principally due to the fact that he was at the notorious card game that became known as the Baccarat scandal. In brief one of the players Sir William Gordon-Cumming, also an officer in the Scots Guards, had been accused of cheating in a game of baccarat at Tranby Croft in Yorkshire in 1890. Initially the matter was kept secret but when the story eventually leaked Sir William sued his accusers for libel with Berkeley Levett being one of the defendants. What had made the scandal so high profile was that the Prince of Wales, the future King Edward VII had been at the card game. The Prince was subsequently required to testify in court. Sir William lost the case and was forced to resign from the regiment even though public sympathy had

The badge of the prestigious Scots Guards

largely been on his side. After the war Berkeley Levett would serve as Gentleman Usher to the Royal Household from 1919 to 1931. It is the same Major Levett who on 29th June 1918 wrote a letter of introduction for Alfred Curphey to Major Law at the recruiting office. The letter, which is on file along with his other army records, states:

'Dear Major Law
The bearer of this has to report on July 1st. I do not know what the procedure of this man of 47 is but I want to state that Mr Alfred Curphey has done and is doing most valuable work under the Ministry of Information and anything you can do to get him with a good regiment would be most kind. We know all about him at these Head Quarters.
Yrs sincerely
Berkeley Levett
Major and a.d.c to Lt. General'

What they actually knew about Alfred Curphey beyond his work in Mexico is probably open to question. In any event a letter dated 5th July 1918 from the Director of Organisation at the War Office to the Assistant Director of Recruiting at Great Scotland Yard SW1 states:

'Sir
I am directed to forward the attached letter authorising the posting of A G Curphey of 16 Suffolk Street, Pall Mall, S.W 1 to the Scots Guards, (with a view to subsequent admission to an Officer Cadet Unit) and request you to attach it to the documents of the man in question when he is handed over to the Military Authorities for posting.
Mr Curphey has been directed to apply to you for instructions regarding attestation.
I am
Sir
Your obedient servant'
The signature on the letter is illegible

Even in wartime it seems remarkable that a 46-year-old man (Berkeley Levett had his age wrong by a year) with no previous military experience should be posted to a prestigious regiment such as the Scots Guards and even more remarkable that he should be recommended for officer training. A Lieutenant Cormack of the Scots Guards clearly thought the same as his application was swiftly rejected. Further strings must have been pulled as only a few days later Alfred Curphey was accepted as a private into the Scots Guards by the same Lieutenant Cormack. His regimental number was 18865.

Alfred's military records add some details about him that had hitherto not been known. Even in an age when photography was less common it is surprising that no photographs of him exist other than one purported to have been amongst the records of the Mellon divorce case. His medical records provide more information about his appearance. Notes from a preliminary examination prior to assignment on 1st July 1918 show his age correctly as 46 years and 3 months but give his place of birth as the Isle of Mann. This information must have been provided by Alfred. His occupation is given as Financial Agent. He is described as being 5ft 10 ½ ins tall and weighing 162 lbs (11 st 8 lbs). Hair colour is given as black with blue eyes and a fresh complexion. His chest measurement was 38 ins and his physical development is described as good with heart and lungs normal. His vision is given as 6/6 in both eyes (equivalent of 20/20). Additional notes state that he has a scar on his right eyebrow and tattoos on both forearms and a tattoo above the heart on his chest.

The tattoo on his chest is interesting as David Cannadine mentions it in his book on Andrew Mellon. According to the deposition by Charles Ernest Long both Alfred and Nora each got tattoos in 1908. Alfred had the name 'Nora' tattooed on his left breast while Nora had the word 'Pig' over her heart. Pig was the pet name that she called Alfred. Nora's son Paul would later dispute this in respect of his mother. The details of the tattoo are not given in Alfred's army records but it does seem to add veracity to Long's statement.

Alfred initially seems to have been categorised as A1 but on the same record, possibly at his subsequent examination for admission to the Scots Guards on 8th July 1918 he is re-categorised as B1.

The difference between the two categories based on the classification used during World War 1 are as follows:

A Able to march, see to shoot, hear well and stand active service conditions
Subcategories:
A1 Fit for dispatching overseas, as regards physical and mental health, and training
A2 As A1, except for training
A3 Returned Expeditionary Force men, ready except for physical condition
A4 Men under 19 who would be A1 or A2 when aged 19

B Free from serious organic diseases, able to stand service on lines of communication in France, or in garrisons in the tropics
Subcategories:
B1 Able to march 5 miles, see to shoot with glasses, and hear well
B2 Able to walk 5 miles, see and hear sufficiently for ordinary purposes
B3 Only suitable for sedentary work

His service record is brief but does add that his next of kin was given as his solicitor Mr E C Oubry, 10 Little College Street, Westminster. Both his parents were dead by this time but his sisters were still alive. This would seem to indicate that he had not maintained contact with his family. Oubry had been his solicitor for his divorce proceedings with Grace so their association had been a long one.

His conduct sheet for his short period of service is clean and shows that he was assigned to the 3rd battalion of the Scots Guards. Having got himself into the prestigious regiment Alfred clearly had no inclination to fight and on 19th September 1918 he is admitted to Caterham hospital. Medical notes on his army record state:

Age 46. Chronic lumbago – on and off for 20 years. Too old for drilling etc in Guards. Banker in civil life and unaccustomed to much physical work.
Rec. B2 T.M.B.

His further re-classification as B2 is confirmed on his medical record on 8th October 1918. Quite how he served the rest of his time in the army is not noted anywhere on his record but he is demobbed on 7th January 1919. His discharge certificate states his theatre of war as London district. He had not been anywhere near the fighting. His address on discharge is given as 16 Suffolk Street, Pall Mall.

CHAPTER 15
THE FINANCIER'S DAUGHTER

Information on what exactly Alfred Curphey was doing in the years after he left the army are somewhat sparse but there are enough details to suggest that the leopard had not necessarily changed his spots and had settled down to a more conventional lifestyle.

At some point in 1919 or early 1920 he has come into contact with a gentleman by the name of James White. In some ways James White was a similar character to Alfred. He too was born in humble surroundings in Rochdale, Lancashire and had worked for a time in a cotton mill as well as spending time as a labourer working on the railway in South Africa. He then turned his hand to being a builder and ventured into buying and selling property. In this venture it seems he overreached himself as he was declared bankrupt in 1908. Unlike Alfred Curphey it was reported that all his creditors were eventually repaid in full.

James next tried his hand as a boxing promoter and this venture proved much more successful for him. A controversial boxing event in 1909 brought him considerable newspaper attention when the event was banned in London because one of the fighters was black. White threatened to take the event to Paris and the consequent attention brought him a growing reputation as a noted wheeler dealer.

In addition to his boxing promotions he also turned his attention to theatre management and owning racehorses. An inveterate gambler he also became a well known property speculator. During the war he also became known through his involvement in the financial affairs of the Beecham family. James had persuaded Sir Joseph Beecham (of Beecham's pills fame) to underwrite the purchase of the Covent garden estate and market in London. The outbreak of war had meant the enterprise had restricted the ability of James White to complete the deal and he was still trying to resolve matters when Sir Joseph died in 1916 and the affair eventually had to be sorted by the courts. James continued to build up a successful racehorse stable and speculate in property and shares after the war ended and it is possible that this is how he and Alfred became acquainted. James White was also involved with the Ministry of Information during the latter years of the war. He was responsible for running the sport and entertainment section and was principally involved with providing entertainment for American troops during the last year of the war. A connection to Alfred Curphey through the Ministry of Information is therefore another possibility.

They may also have come to know each other through James White's elder daughter Celia as she and Alfred Curphey became engaged in 1920. Whether Alfred got to know Celia through his association with James White or got to know James through Celia, the pair were married on 22nd September 1920 at the St Georges district registry office in Hannover Square, London. His wife Celia, whose address is given as 36 Latham Road, Southport, Lancashire, was only 21 years old. In fact Alfred is five years older than his new father in law.

Unlike the information on his first marriage certificate, this time Alfred's details appear to be correct. His age is correctly stated as 48 years old and he is described as the divorced husband of Grace Dundas Hamilton Souter Curphey formerly Robertson. His father is correctly described as Samuel Curphey (deceased) although there is a bit of licence in describing his father, a former joiner, as having been of independent means. Alfred's address is given as the Washington Hotel, Curzon Street, W1. His occupation is given as Financial Agent and in a move more true to his nature the words 'ex Army' are added in brackets. At this time, virtually every man getting married in England could probably claim to be ex Army or Navy so it is a touch flamboyant to add these details to the marriage certificate, particularly as Alfred's brief army career had predominantly been spent in Caterham hospital suffering from chronic lumbago!

James must have trusted his new son in law as in 1921 Alfred is one of three trustees named in a settlement made by James White to his wife Annie upon their divorce of £60,000 to provide an annuity of £4,200 per annum before tax. The other trustees are named as Charles John Hall and Richard Cobbett both from Manchester.

The newly married couple seemed to have lived at Datchet Cottage at Datchet, Windsor. Alfred is listed as living at that address in Kelly's directory of 1924. It would seem that he had grown fond of the area around Windsor from the time spent there with Nora Mellon. Datchet Cottage still exists in a semi rural area on Sandlea Road, Datchet. While it has probably been extended since the 1920s it is still a pleasant and quite large property although nowhere near as palatial as the surroundings Alfred had enjoyed while at Ballamoar Castle on the Isle of Man.

Celia Curphey had also given this address as her place of residence when arriving in New York from Southampton on board the Majestic in March 1923. The purpose of her visit is not known but Alfred was not with her. Her travelling companion is Norma Leahy of 11 Albert Hall Mansions, London.

Datchet Cottage is still the address given for an entry in the London Gazette of 14th December 1926 relating to the proposed registration of a leasehold title. The property in question is described as leasehold land and buildings 1-5 (all) The Parade and the Kilburn Empire, High Road, Kilburn. The registered proprietor is given as Celia Curphey of Datchet Cottage, Datchet, Bucks. As mentioned previously her father had an interest in theatres and in 1922 he had acquired a controlling interest in Daly's theatre in Westminster. The purchase of the Kilburn Empire and adjoining properties could have been a venture undertaken by James White but using his daughter as the means to do so. It could equally have been a venture undertaken jointly by the Curpheys or indeed just a venture made by Celia in her own right. Whatever the situation, the day to day running of the theatre was left to a gentleman by the name of Charles Gulliver.

On 29th June 1927 things took a dramatic and tragic turn when James White was found dead at his home in Wiltshire having committed suicide. It would very soon come to light that the inveterate speculator and gambler had taken one gamble too many and was facing a substantial number of debts that he could not hope to resolve.

It was stated that his affairs were in a highly involved state and that there were enormous debts. The news caused ripples at the London Stock Exchange and a consequent dip in share prices. There was widespread concern that the extensive dealings that James White had undertaken with numerous firms on the Stock Exchange could cause some of them to fail to meet their own obligations. This concern proved not to be the case although for a period there was also a worry that James White had numerous friends and followers who might also now be exposed to debt. It is not known if Alfred Curphey was among the followers. If so on this occasion he seems to have escaped the bankruptcy court.

An inquest into the death of James White was held at his home on 1st July 1927. There was considerable press interest and the members of the press were not happy at having to wait outside in torrential rain until the inquest was convened. A note had been left to his doctor stating 'Go easy with me old man. I am dead from prussic acid. No need to cut any deeper – Jimmy'. In fact the inquest determined that death had been caused by chloroform poisoning and the jury returned a verdict of suicide while insane.

The funeral was held on 4th July 1927 with a great many in attendance, including some well known names from the world of racing and theatre. Contemporary reports briefly mention that his two daughters from his first marriage (Celia and Agnes) viewed the flowers left by well wishers. Alfred Curphey presumably attended with Celia.

It soon became clear that liabilities running to several hundreds of thousands far outweighed any assets and that unsecured creditors would be left with nothing. This included his second wife and the children from that marriage. The trust settled in favour of his first wife Annie in 1921 was unaffected by his death and the subsequent fallout. This is known due to a court case from March 1928 at which Alfred Curphey was present as one of the trustees of the settlement. The case related to whether James White's former wife Annie (now Annie Culshaw) was entitled to the money gross or net of tax.

The repercussions following on from the death of James White rumbled on for some time. As reported in Hansard on 31st January 1929, a question concerning his affairs was asked of the Chancellor of the Exchequer (Winston Churchill) by Lord Henry Cavendish Bentinck as follows:

'asked the Chancellor of the Exchequer whether he is aware that the late Mr. James White, financier, of Foxhill, Swindon, died having paid no Income Tax or Super-tax from 1921 till the time of his death in 1927, and that the amounts due to the Crown were approximately £1,700,000; whether it is a common practice to allow a man to avoid all payment of taxes for six years; and, if not, why Mr. James White was so allowed?'

The reply from Winston Churchill was:

'My Noble Friend has been misinformed. It is true that large assessments—though not so large as he suggests—were outstanding at the time of Mr. James White's death, but they were merely in estimated amounts in the absence of a return and were under appeal; and Mr. White made a substantial payment on account shortly before his death. My Noble Friend will of course realise that exceptional difficulty attends the collection of tax from people who make and lose great fortunes in quick succession and keep no accounts, and he must not draw any general inferences. Even in this case I am informed that the interests of the Revenue have been substantially safeguarded.' (Hansard Volume 224 Column 1128 31st January 1929)

As James White's second wife Doris and their children were left virtually penniless it is probable that there were no funds available to his daughters Celia and Agnes from the first marriage.

For Alfred the loss of his formerly wealthy father in law must have been a blow but there is nothing to show what the repercussions were for him. In 1930 he is involved in a land deal in Ashton under Lyme where he is mentioned in a sale of land by Thomas Mason & Sons Ltd to Lord Estates Ltd. In the sale details he is listed alongside the names of the solicitors as a stockbroker.

His life had presumably continued as normal... but it would not be for long!

CHAPTER 16

A PHILANDERER IS CUCKOLDED

By March 1932 Alfred Curphey found himself once again in familiar surroundings, namely the divorce courts. This time however the shoe was on the other the foot and Alfred was petitioning for divorce on the grounds of Celia's adultery with a gentleman by the name of John Bushby.

Few details are given beyond the various legal documents necessary for the proceedings. The divorce petition is filed on 11th March 1932. Alfred's address is given as New Court, Middle Temple, London and his profession is still stated as Financial Agent.

The documents confirm that the pair were married on 22nd September 1920 and had lived at various places but principally Datchet Cottage, Datchet and that there were no children from the marriage.

Celia's address is given as 189 Boulevard Bineau, Neuilly, Paris and the petition alleged that she had lived there since at least 9th April 1931 in co-habitation with John Bushby with whom she had regularly committed adultery.

A lady by the name of Anne Haselden is cited as a witness but her testimony is not recorded with the divorce documentation. Summons were issued to both Celia Curphey and John Bushby either to appear in person or appoint a solicitor to appear on their behalf but the divorce appears to have been uncontested and a decree nisi was granted on 7th November 1932 with a decree absolute following on 19th June 1933.

One aspect that is striking when reviewing Alfred Curphey's life is that there is no evidence that he fathered any children. He was married to Grace for 12 years and was living with her for 10 years from 1893 before moving out of the family home in 1903 yet the divorce papers make it clear that there was no issue from the marriage. Similarly he was married to Celia from 1920 until 1933 and the divorce papers show that she was not with John Bushby until 1931. Again the divorce papers show that there were no children from the marriage.

He also had numerous affairs, with the mysterious Alice as cited in the papers for his first divorce, with Lady Vivian and with Nora Mellon on two different occasions. There will very probably have been many other liaisons. While not conclusive this would tend to indicate that he could not have children. Nora Mellon conceived two children with Andrew Mellon while Lady Vivian also had two children with her first husband the 4th Baron Vivian so it could have been very possible for them to have had a child by Alfred.

CHAPTER 17

A MYSTERY TO THE END

Following his divorce it is again difficult to find any information on Alfred's whereabouts or what he was up to over the next few years. His first wife Grace died in 1933 in Wiltshire although it is unlikely that Alfred would have even known about this given they had been divorced for almost 30 years. When his name does reappear it is once again in surprising circumstances. He is named as an executor for the will of a gentleman by the name of George Beldam.

George Beldam was also a very colourful character who was born in 1868 just a few years before Alfred. He graduated from Peterhouse College, Cambridge with a degree in Engineering. A talented all round sportsman he played football for Brentford FC but more notably he played first class cricket for Middlesex from 1900 to 1907. He represented the Gentlemen versus the Players on a couple of occasions. He also reportedly taught the legendary cricketer W G Grace how to play golf!

He was an avid inventor, amongst his inventions being the Beldam tyre but following his retirement from cricket he became most noted for his work in the sphere of action photography, particularly with regard to cricket and golf. He collaborated on a couple of books with the noted cricketer C B Fry and his action photographs were highly regarded. He was also a well respected artist specialising in water colours.

His private life was also very colourful. He was first married to Gertrude Cottam in 1892. This marriage ended in divorce and he subsequently married a much younger woman named Margaret Underwood in 1921. This too ended in divorce and in 1930 he married Christina Thomson. Christina was some 37 years younger than him and indeed was some 8 years younger than his daughter Kathleen from his first marriage.

George Beldam died of a heart attack at his home Rhodendale near Farnham in Surrey on 23rd November 1937. The three executors named in his will are Albon Tabor Austin Dobson CVO CBE, a senior civil servant but also a former cricketer, a solicitor named Thomas James Worley and Alfred George Curphey. In this instance Alfred is stated to be an engineer which perhaps explains his link to George Beldam.

Alfred does seem to have had an interest in engineering, particularly relating to railways. In 1904 he was listed as the joint holder of a patent for electric railway signalling equipment in Adelaide, South Australia even though he does not appear to have visited that part of the world. His pretext for his initial loan from Andrew Mellon was also related to the railways. There is also correspondence from Alfred Curphey to Henry Frick (a lifelong friend of Andrew Mellon) inviting him to view a model railway that Alfred stated was at No 307, Fifth Avenue. New York. Frick's response is polite but distant even though the correspondence dates from February 1903 before the scandal of Alfred's affair with Nora became known. It is therefore likely that he and George Beldam became acquainted by means of their mutual interest in engineering. In April 1938 probate was granted on the will of George Beldam with effects in the sum of £42,234 – 4s – 4d.

Alfred Curphey did not live much longer after this and he died on 4th October 1938 at the age of 66 years. The cause of death was certified by W W Jenkin M.B. as carcinoma of bronchus, a variant of lung cancer. He died at the former home of George Beldam, Rhodendale, Lower Bourne, Farnham. He had presumably been living there with Christine, Beldam's third wife, which might beg the question whether his friendship had been entirely with George Beldam or also with his wife.

George Beldam

After all the various times he had made newspaper headlines, including during his brief spell on the Isle of Man it is only the *Ramsey Courier* of 14th October 1938 that takes note of his demise:

'MR A G CURPHEY DEAD
'FORMER OWNER OF BALLAMOAR
'News is just to hand of the death which occurred in a London nursing home of Mr A.G. Curphey, formerly of Ballamoar, Jurby.

'Mr Curphey will be remembered as a picturesque figure by many Ramsey people. He lived in style at Ballamoar for a number of years, and in his heyday gave away considerable sums of money to charitable objects. He was largely interested in an Egyptian shipping company and had many other business interests. He was married to a daughter of the late Mr "Jimmy" White, financier. He was succeeded at Ballamoar by the late Mr J. D. Blackwell'

There is no record of his funeral, nor are any details of a will or his estate to be found. It is quite possible that he was once again without funds and had been living on the goodwill of Christina Beldam at the time of his death. His name on the death certificate was corrected to Curphey on 12th March 1941 on production of a statutory declaration from Thomas James Worley and Leslie Charles Toms. As Thomas Worley was also a named executor together with Alfred Curphey under the will of George Beldam, this correction was presumably made to formalise matters relating to the Beldam estate.

There is, however, a strange footnote to Alfred Curphey's death. In his book, 'Mellon, An American Life', David Cannadine makes a brief reference to a letter found in the papers of David E Koskoff. Koskoff had written an earlier biography of Andrew Mellon. The letter is dated 7th October 1977 and is from someone by the name of K G Raffield to David Koskoff. In this letter it is stated that some twenty years after his death, Alfred Curphey's ashes were scattered at Three Legged Cross in Dorset by Christina Beldam. From a timing perspective this is possible. Christina Beldam lived to the age of 64, dying in 1969 at Worplesdon near Guildford in Surrey. She did not remarry. Rhodendale was sold by the remaining executors to her late husband's estate in April 1939 so she had presumably taken Alfred's ashes with her when she left Rhodendale and in any subsequent moves over the following twenty years!

Quite why she suddenly decided to scatter his ashes at this point is never going to be known. Equally strange is that she chose to scatter them at a place known as Three Legged Cross. Alfred had no known association with the place as far as can be ascertained.

It is quite possible that she chose the place based on the name, in some way identifying it with the three legs of Man, the ancient symbol of the Isle of Man as depicted on the Manx flag. It would seem that the final resting place of Alfred George Curphey is as mysterious and intriguing as had been his life.